HELPING OTHERS GROW THROUGH
MENTOR-BASED LEADERSHIP

DR. C. D. DUDLEY

HELPING OTHERS GROW THROUGH
MENTOR-BASED LEADERSHIP

DR. C. D. DUDLEY

© 2022 C. D. Dudley

All rights reserved.

No part of this publication may be reproduced, stored in a retrieval system or transmitted in any form or by any means, electronic, mechanical, photocopying, recording or otherwise, without the expressed written permission of the publisher.

Scripture references are taken from various versions and translations of the Holy Bible. Pronouns for referring to the Father, Son and Holy Spirit are capitalized intentionally and the words satan and devil are never capitalized.

Publisher:
MEWE, LLC
www.mewellc.com

BLOOM
First Edition
ISBN: 978-1-7360565-8-5

Library of Congress Control Number: 2022947202

Printed in the United States of America.

This book is dedicated to every Bloom Leader who is committed to the growth and development of others through acceptance, appreciation, admiration (respect), advisement, and advancement.
Thank you for being committed to the…BLOOM.

Table of Content

Acknowledgements ix
Preface xi
    Leading Like Jesus xiii
    Mentor-based Leadership xiv
    Introducing Bloom Leadership xv
    Book Overview xvi

PART I – Desiring a Greater Impact

Chapter One – A New Type of Leadership 3
    Influence vs. Power 4
    See the Value in Others 6
    Serve with Love 7
Chapter Two – Bloom `Leadership 11
    Existing Leadership Theories 12
    Bloom Leadership Element 1 – Acceptance 15
    Bloom Leadership Element 2 – Appreciation 20
    Bloom Leadership Element 3 – Admiration (Respect) 25
    Bloom Leadership Element 4 – Advisement 29
    Bloom Leadership Element 5 – Advancement 33
Chapter Three – Leaders Leading Leaders 39
    Lead with a Parent-like Nature 41
    Mentor Sons and Daughters 42
    Be an Example of Excellent Leadership 43
    Allow Others to Also Lead 44

PART II – Preparing for Change

Chapter Four – Becoming a Culture Change Agent 51
    Understanding the Impact of Culture 52
    Know Your Climate 55
    The Emperor vs. the Gardener 56
    Bruise and Bandage Mentality of Leaders 60
    Gossiping Destroys Good Culture 62
    Sparking Culture Change 63

Chapter Five – Now and Later 67
    Defining Your Organization 68
    Making Your Vision and Mission Known 69
    Establishing a Plan 71
    Collaboration vs. Comparison 74

PART III – Moving Beyond Challenges

Chapter Six – Overcoming Offenses 79
    Don't Take the Bait of Offense 80
    The Path to Forgiveness 82
    Keeping Your Mind at Peace 85
    Looking at Negative Experiences Differently 86

Epilogue 91
    Teach Like Jesus 92
    The Five-Step Process of Training 93
    The Benefit of the Bloom 94

Endnotes 97
About the Author 99
Other Products 101

Acknowledgements

I want to thank my oldest daughter, Hannah, for helping me to organize all of my notes, outlines, audio files and transcripts so that I could turn my ideas and concepts into a book. Compiling information that I had presented over several years was a huge undertaking. You are an exceptional project manager. I want to thank my middle daughter, Taylor, for helping me brand the Bloom Leadership concept and present myself in the best way to others. You are a talented writer and marketing expert.

I am also thankful for the inspiration and support from E. Robinson. You helped me to frame the concept of Bloom Leadership, and you took the time to help me present the elements, in excellence, to ministry leaders in our community. I appreciate you for sharing your gifts of leadership, communication, planning, and innovation.

Thank you to my former supervisor, the Late Dr. B. Johnson, for teaching me how to lead others through your example of excellence and honor; and thank you to the Late Dr. P. Starnes for approving me to take risks as a workforce development leader and for publicly recognizing me for my efforts. I quote both of these illustrious leaders often on my leadership journey. I am grateful for their impact.

Thank you to every person who invited me to speak at your company, non-profit, church, event, conference, or family gathering. It all played a vital part in my growth and development. You were (are) committed to my BLOOM.

Preface

I began researching and eventually writing this book to connect some of the pieces in my life together and to be able to express my feelings about negative organizational culture and how to get to a better place. Surprisingly, I found that toxic interactions had a bigger influence on culture than most of the well-organized plans that organizations could establish. After some of my experiences, I needed some time to reflect and reposition myself not just as a leader with a number of publications, productions, and programs, but as someone who could speak for others who, like me, have been hurt within organizations and who want to lead and be led in a way that stems from respect. I understood that change had to begin with me. So, I started on my BLOOM mission.

Through my faith, years of research, and both positive and negative experiences, I have learned that the process of leadership can be improved when leaders are willing to put aside their own interests and purposefully focus on valuing and serving others. This is accomplished by cultivating a relationship based on mutual respect, guidance, and development, which improves satisfaction and productivity. Overall, Jesus is my primary example when it comes to leadership, which entails showing followers and leaders how to respectfully interact while working toward a common objective. The "Jesus way" has emerged as the most effective way, despite all the conclusions I have drawn from my research and the numerous analyses of empirical literature. Since Jesus is the most influential leader in my life, I dare not leave Him out of this discussion.

Now, I want you to keep a few things in mind as you read through the book. First, the terms workplace, organization, business, church, and work environment are used interchangeably as places where interactions between leaders and followers occur.

Second, the term *leader* describes someone who is in a higher position of authority or an individual who influences and inspires others towards the vision of an organization. The term *follower* is used to describe an individual in a lower position or someone who desires to be influenced by a leader. It is important to note that a follower can also be a leader who is influenced by another leader in a higher position of authority.

Third, in some parts of the book, I speak specifically to leaders in an attempt to help them transform their style of leading to a more mentor-based way; and in other parts of the book, I am speaking to both leaders and followers concerning principles essential to interacting with others, in general, and also moving past negative interactions.

Leading Like Jesus

From a spiritual sense, leadership is the capacity to emulate Jesus' teaching and thereby empower and equip those around you. A mentoring leaders' success can be measured by seeing if the mentee, follower, or protégé has reproduced or enhanced other leaders – leaders who have been nurtured and developed during their relationship. Leaders must be willing to not only lead strongly through a combination of mentoring and role modeling, but they must also be willing to delegate, which follows Jesus' example, *"And he saith unto them, Follow me, and I will make you fishers of men"* (Matthew 4:19). Note that Jesus' call to His disciples to "follow" and be "fishers of men," speaks of shared responsibilities. With this kind of delegation, the leader can inspire the mentee to be passionate and confident. Take a look at how the disciples responded, *"Did not our heart burn within us, while he talked with us by the way, and while he opened to us the scriptures?"* (Luke 24:32, emphasis added).

The disciples' faith increased as a result of Jesus' leadership, and they learned to trust Him more and more over time. They became not only receptive to Jesus' teachings, but also inspired to put what they had learned into action. In that passion, they realized they didn't have to live in fear of failure. As a result, we see a gradual improvement in the disciples' abilities throughout the New Testament. This transformation was most visible in Peter, who was able to preach the word and eager to serve wherever he was called. While the Holy Spirit did empower the disciples at Pentecost, their readiness to be equipped is due to Jesus' commitment to their training when He walked with them. (See Acts 2:1-41).

The disciples were shown an example of true servant leadership and mentoring through the influence of Jesus. This is our benchmark, and we should always strive to serve others. Above all, Jesus spent a significant amount of time teaching the disciples about interactions and relationships. Jesus also showed the disciples how to treat one another and people from all walks of life, whether they were servants or centurions, Jews or Gentiles. It's no different in organizations. Leaders communicate their expectations in terms of productivity, goals and objectives, and qualities. However, one of the expectations that is frequently overlooked is how people should interact with one another. Leaders specifically fail to address how they will treat each other or devise an interpersonal communication strategy. When leaders do not make such things plain, they have to deal with all sorts of conflicts and misunderstandings as they arise.

I want you to think about the fact that Jesus spent a lot of time teaching His disciples how they should treat others in human interaction, and how that lesson yielded hundred-fold results. One person, Jesus, served as the foundation of the gospel. Jesus then trained twelve, who then started training other disciples. As a result, billions of people have accepted Christ. Wow! One leader and a small group of followers were the beginning of this enormous amount of growth. Because of Jesus' servant leadership, the disciples and others followed Him out of love rather than resentment or fear. We have the essence of human interaction and its power to multiply when we learn how to treat one another.

Mentor-based Leadership

Traditional mentoring occurs when an individual who is more experienced makes a commitment to guide another individual in obtaining the knowledge and skills necessary for development or promotion. According to Kram (1983), mentors are key to providing various supportive behaviors or functions as the mentees carry out tasks that spur the development necessary to advance inside and outside of the workplace. This book is focused more on the biblical foundation of leadership and mentoring, which was important to me because of my faith. Later, I will publish a book that includes a plethora of citations from my own academic research study and empirical articles from other scholars.

Present-day leadership should evolve towards becoming more a more mentor-based, which consists of principles from various leadership theories, including transformational, servant, and leader/member exchange. Particularly, the concept of the transformational leadership theory sees leaders moving from mere commanding, directing, and supervising to guiding, delegating, developing, and respecting. With this in mind, leaders should be more concerned about the well-being, growth, and progression of others.

Moving from a centralized environment to a more decentralized environment, where more people are involved in decision making processes also aids in growth and development. Some time ago, leadership meant, "Do what I say," or "I make the decisions, and you carry them out." But as leadership transitions to becoming more mentor-based and team-oriented, the presence and participation of followers are welcomed by leaders in positions of authority. Relationships improve and more opportunities are presented for followers to develop and grow. The servant leadership style primarily involves the leader adopting a servant or mentor-based mindset instead of focusing on dictating to followers. As more leaders are learning to lead like Jesus, followers are guided, equipped, coached, trained, and assured they are not just parts in a machine. Interactions improve as a result of leaders spending more time with followers and committing to meeting their needs. Moreover, the interactions between leaders and followers shape an organization's climate or culture, whether for the better or worse. Therefore, if you want to improve the culture within the organization, you must improve the interactions. Followers or members will feel "good," as studies show, about their presence and their contributions to the organization.

Again, an intrinsic part of leadership is mentoring. In a traditional sense, this is the position where someone in a more senior position, with more experience, commits to investing time and effort in the growth of someone in a lower position. This MUST stem from a real desire to see others advance within their roles, personally and professionally. Just think of the different roles you've held in the past. If your boss or supervisor had made a commitment to your growth, how would it have changed your experience and upward momentum in that career? What if every workplace had a mentoring culture? In today's society, mentoring takes many different forms, including traditional mentoring, peer mentoring, network mentoring, group mentoring and so on. However, the essence is still the same – the desire to see others grow or bloom, which is the foundation of Bloom Leadership.

Introducing Bloom Leadership

The title "Bloom Leader" speaks of development and growth because when a flower blooms, it grows from a bud to its fullest potential of beauty. To this end, a Bloom Leader is a person in leadership who has made a commitment to help someone else develop and grow through mentor-based behavior or functions. Positive interactions lead to a more positive culture. Positive culture drives performance, and performance drives success. This leads me to introduce the five elements of Bloom Leadership, which are designed to improve interactions within an organization.

1. Acceptance (affirming, welcoming)
2. Appreciation (incentive, motivation, praise)
3. Admiration (respect, honor)

4. Advisement (mentoring, coaching, guiding)
5. Advancement (training, empowerment, opportunities)

All five elements can be applied to different organizational dyads, which include leader-follower, leader-leader, and follower-follower; however, this book will focus on the first two types, involving leaders. Although all five elements improve interactions to promote a positive culture, the Advisement element is a model of how interactions in leader-leader dyads may be strengthened. The biblical example of Paul mentoring Timothy, who was also a leader, provides insights for senior leaders deciding to pivot from a style that is directing, commanding, and instructing to one that includes more mentoring, guidance, respect, and empowerment. We will see how Paul and Timothy's relationship provides an unmatched example of this crucial element.

Book Overview

As we progress in exploring leadership throughout the chapters of this book, we will focus on:

- Examining a new type of mentor-based leadership
- Describing the five elements of Bloom Leadership
- Explaining the concept of 'leaders leading leaders'
- Creating a positive culture
- Defining the foundational aspects of organizations
- Overcoming offenses and 'going back in' after negative situations

Please understand that interacting with others effectively and respectfully is critical to successful leadership and positive culture. Yes, we all make mistakes occasionally because no one is perfect. However, our deepest desire should be to value others and see them grow. By taking this journey through the pages of this book, you are on your way to becoming a better leader – more committed to helping others BLOOM…

PART 1

Desiring a Greater Impact

ONE

A New Type of Leadership

BLOOM

It's a truism, but you cannot be a leader unless you have followers, aside from managing your own life to become a better version of yourself. And the goal of great leaders should be to influence others to help achieve established goals. Leaders who are committed to developing and growing others through respect are better capable of achieving their goals. Why? Because environments that promote growth and respect make people happier and more productive. Let's delve deeper.

Influence vs. Power

You see, leadership is all about influence. The efficacy of how we inspire and direct others toward success reveals our capacity as good leaders. As a Christian leader, this is done by emulating the teachings of Jesus, the ultimate example of a true leader. He didn't simply exercise His power to lead, as so many leaders do in today's world. Instead, Jesus led by His influence. According to the Bible, thousands of people were moved to follow Jesus for days on end, not only as a result of His teachings but also as a result of the caring ways He displayed for even the least of them.

> *In those days the multitude being very great, and having nothing to eat, Jesus called his disciples unto him, and saith unto them, I have compassion on the multitude, because they have now been with me three days, and have nothing to eat: And if I send them away fasting to their own houses, they will faint by the way: for divers of them came from far* (Mark 8:1-3).

Leadership is not about raw power. You have probably seen the boss in the workplace who takes pleasure in crushing others' morale with the weight of their authority. That is not the kind of leadership that empowers and motivates others, and it is certainly not the kind of leadership that Jesus showed in His ministry. In fact, someone without the power that comes with a position may have more influence than someone who has been appointed to a position of authority. That tells me that people who are in positions of authority may or may not be true leaders or influencers of others.

I have learned through my leadership positions over the years that everyone deserves respect, from people in entry-level positions to those in the boardroom. Leading by power doesn't allow you to accord the respect to each individual that they deserve. You shouldn't want to foster a culture where people only follow you out of obligation or in exchange for favors or benefits. Instead, you should want to foster an atmosphere in which people genuinely want to follow you because you have had such a positive impact on their behavior and thinking. This hammers home the fact that successful leadership is not about gaining followers but rather about having a substantial effect on people – the type of effect that causes satisfaction, growth, and development.

It is a myth to think that only leaders are important in the process of leadership. No. Followers are essential to the frontline and to the overall mission and vision of the organization as their feedback is crucial to fully understanding the changes or improvements that need to take place. Furthermore, followers may shoulder the responsibility of encouraging their peers to support the organization's goals. Even in a follower role, individuals may deport themselves as opinion leaders, thus having impact in creating a better organizational culture through positive, affirming interactions. It is by cooperating with the leader that followers can prepare for a formal leadership role in the future. Both followers and leaders should respond appropriately when interacting with each other for their relationships to be positive and effective.

I remember joining an organization and attending a monthly meeting for the first time. I had not been told by the person who invited me about the necessary protocols regarding attire and I assumed because it was a Saturday meeting that I could dress casually. I recall a lady coming up to me and tapping me on the shoulder. She quietly said, "Excuse me, but business attire is appropriate for this month's meeting. Do you have anything else that you can wear?" I responded, "You know what? I do. I have some extra clothes in my trunk."

She did not make scene or bring attention to the situation. I could have gotten angry and made the situation much bigger than it needed to be if I had not been a good follower. But she was gracious to me; so, I resolved to being generous in return. As she explained the protocol, I decided to show her respect and honor. This resulted in a positive interaction, which is accomplished by both the follower and the leader doing their part. Positive interactions are essential for fostering a healthy organizational culture.

If you want to improve the culture, you must improve the interactions, paving the way for Bloom Leadership.

BLOOM

See the Value in Others

Quality leadership also entails seeing others as valuable. To help me with this, I try to be intentional about treating others as if they were royalty. Royalty, indeed. When I imagine others as kings or queens, I better understand that they are worthy of my respect. I reshape my priorities to have a servant's heart in order to motivate them to be and do their best. This does wonders for morale. When we look around today's organizations, we can see many people struggling to find their self-worth. God can use us to be a source of encouragement to them. When we treat others with respect, we should gain respect in return. This allows us the opportunity to influence the other person. People prefer to work with leaders who make them feel valued and respected. Believe it or not, they develop a desire to impress you, to please you, and work at their optimum.

> *Quality leadership also entails seeing others as valuable.*

Outstanding leadership starts with how we view people, considering what would benefit them the most. This is a far cry from the "I, me and my" culture of today where "loving myself only" is a kind of obsession. We cannot stop at just loving ourselves and desiring others to also love us. Jesus encourages us to love God, ourselves, and our neighbors.

> *Master, which is the great commandment in the law? Jesus said unto him, Thou shalt love the Lord thy God with all thy heart, and with all thy soul, and with all thy mind. This is the first and great commandment. And the second is like unto it, Thou shalt love thy neighbour as thyself. On these two commandments hang all the law and the prophets* (Matthew 22:36-40).

In this "loving myself" and "love me" culture, Jesus taught us to be counter-cultural, focusing on others' needs before our own. This is servant and transformational leadership. Jesus practiced servant leadership all throughout His life right up till His death. He didn't need to go to the cross, but He knew we needed a Savior. Mark 10:45 reads, "*For even the Son of man came not to be ministered unto, but to minister, and to give his life a ransom for many.*" Are you willing to see the value in others and invest time in helping them to fulfill their calling?

A NEW TYPE OF LEADERSHIP

Serve with Love

Paul, writing to the church in Galatia, calls them to serve one another in love. *"For, brethren, ye have been called unto liberty; only use not liberty for an occasion to the flesh, but by love serve one another"* (Galatians 5:13). We, too, are to serve one another in love, regardless of where we find ourselves, even in organizations. In the workplace, we collaborate with others to achieve the same goals and objectives. To be an effective team member, we must genuinely care about the other person and be willing to serve them in our role. This is frequently difficult because not everyone we encounter is easy to work with. We are often not naturally inclined to like someone due to differences in personalities or the other person's quirks – not to mention our own. How can we love one another when we are dealing with difficult people?

Galatians 5 has wisdom in this area, *"For all the law is fulfilled in one word, even in this; Thou shalt love thy neighbour as thyself. But if ye bite and devour one another, take heed that ye be not consumed one of another"* (Galatians 5:14-15). How regularly do we see this kind of situation in our organizations? Almost every workplace has a few people with a toxic attitude, and this can infect an entire operation and create an atmosphere of strife, which can lower morale.

How do we treat people who we find genuinely hard to work with? Our flesh or worldly self urges us to *"devour one another,"* as it says in Galatians 5:15. When met with negativity and harsh words, our survival instinct is to be defensive and meet fire with fire. If we allow ourselves to do that, we will create an environment that is even more toxic.

On the other hand, we are encouraged by Paul, *"This I say then, Walk in the Spirit, and ye shall not fulfill the lust of the flesh"* (Galatians 5:16). The Spirit calls us to love and practice humility and patience: these are the tools that we need to counter the offenses. We should meet fire with water. You will be amazed at how these qualities can diffuse someone's attitude and cool off a heated situation before it escalates.

What are the other qualities of the Spirit? *"But the fruit of the Spirit is love, joy, peace, longsuffering, gentleness, goodness, faith, meekness, temperance: against such, there is no law"* Paul continues (Galatians 5:22-23). Of course, when faced with negativity, these actions go against our natural inclinations but envisage how different our attitudes and those of people around us would be if we reacted with such gentleness instead!

Imagine this scenario. You walk into the office one day and greet your coworker, who suddenly goes into a tirade about how he is overworked and under-appreciated by management for his hard work. How do you respond? Do you merely nod your head and agree with him, fueling those negative thoughts? Do you ignore him and make him feel like nobody listens to him, increasing his victim mentality? Or do you walk in the Spirit when faced with a situation like this and actually listen? Note that this co-worker does not report to you, but, because he trusts you enough to share his struggles; you have an opportunity to influence him in a positive way.

What if we considered the actual needs of this person, the real problem underlying their frustrations? In this case, it may be the fact that his work is overwhelming him, and he is running behind on his workload, or it may be a personal issue. We will be able to react appropriately if we take a step back and wait for the guidance of the Spirit. If approved or allowed, the Spirit may have us offer to assist him with a project or perhaps take something off his plate in order to help him get back on track. During the process, we could look for mentoring opportunities to teach him skills that will allow him to prioritize his workflow more efficiently and not wind up in the same frustrating place again. Responding in this way allows us to look into our hearts and find empathy. It is possible that we will no longer see him as that annoying coworker who spreads negativity in the workplace, but as a valuable individual who is struggling to keep afloat and needs some assistance. Showing concern or care for others can change the entire environment drastically and support the notion that we do not have to have a title or position to lead or influence others.

> *Showing concern or care for others can change the entire environment drastically...*

Having the mindset to look closer for the real issue is not just appropriate within organizations but for every situation we encounter. Take a moment to think of how responding to others like this could impact your relationships. What if you responded in this way to your spouse or kids? Those relationships would surely bloom. How about the other members of your local church? Those relationships would bloom as well. Your example will be one that other people will naturally want to emulate and adopt for themselves

A NEW TYPE OF LEADERSHIP

because your actions have influenced them louder than your words. You have displayed exceptional leadership…a new type of leadership…by viewing a negative situation as an opportunity to influence and initiate change – you have, in essence, initiated…a bloom!

"True leadership is not about control; it's about service."

– Myles Monroe

TWO

BLOOM LEADERSHIP

BLOOM

Hebrews 6:10 states, *"For God is not unrighteous to forget your work and labour of love, which ye have shewed toward his name, in that ye have ministered to the saints, and do minister."* God will remember what we do for others as we are serving according to His Word in Christ-like character. In the term "Bloom Leadership," the word "bloom" means "to flourish" or "to come into full beauty or health." As a Bloom Leader, your goal is to help people in your organization flourish. If you want your organization to be successful, you must create the type of culture that is healthy and causes people to develop. I have heard it said that "culture trumps all of your systems." No matter how great your plan, it will crumble under the weight of negative culture. Oftentimes, the problems are in areas that are unwritten just as the rules of culture are largely unwritten. Those things that people have adapted and accepted are the very things that govern how they behave and how they think within an organization – this is the meaning of culture.

The title "Bloom Leader" speaks of development and growth. When a flower blooms, it grows from a bud to its fullest potential of beauty. To this end, a Bloom Leader is a person in leadership who has made a commitment to help someone else develop and grow through the five elements of Acceptance, Appreciation, Admiration, Advisement, and Advancement. We shall examine these elements in this chapter. We will also look at how Bloom Leadership is a composite of different leadership theories and explore the key elements of Bloom Leadership using illustrations from the Bible. These elements were created to enhance interactions within organizations. Jesus is our ultimate example. He showed the disciples how to treat people both inside and outside of their inner circle. He knew that treating people appropriately and teaching others how to do the same were just as important as reaching the goal.

> *No matter how great your plan, it will crumble under the weight of negative culture.*

Existing Leadership Theories

According to research, organizations can use guidance, coaching, and mentoring to help mentees develop their people skills, embrace new challenges, avoid potential pitfalls, and develop their leadership abilities. Traditional mentoring occurs when a more experienced individual commits to guiding another individual in acquiring the knowledge and skills required for promotion or development. According to

Kram (1983), mentors are key to providing various supportive behaviors or functions as the mentees carry out tasks that spur the development necessary to advance in the workplace. Some popular leadership theories consist of mentoring functions or behaviors.

Scholars have also explored the phenomenon of leadership, examining the style, traits, and skills of leaders, as well as the responsibility, productivity, and satisfaction of followers. As a result, several models and theories have been revealed that have been useful in both academic and professional settings. Three theories focus more on the development of the follower as opposed to an examination of the leader in the process of leadership. Transformational, servant, and leader/member exchange leadership styles embrace different aspects of mentoring and promote a culture of improvement, growth, and leadership development. More details about these styles are below. Thus, organizations should consider establishing various forms of mentoring methods and training leaders on how to incorporate mentoring behaviors into their leadership styles.

- **Transformational** – this theory postulates that followers are motivated when they have opportunities to be developed or transformed into leaders. Furthermore, this theory suggests that leaders establish relationships with followers that are cultivating, nurturing, and developing in order to change the environment.
- **Servant** – this leadership theory closely resembles the example of Jesus in that the focus of the leader is on developing a trusting relationship with followers as well as identifying and meeting their needs.
- **Leader/Member Exchange (LMX)** – this theory focuses on the different relationships that evolve between leaders and followers. Although leaders commit to a mentoring relationship with some members of the team, all members should be treated with mentor-based behavior.

During the process of completing my doctoral degree in Organizational Leadership, I discovered a need, based upon our society's less traditional work environments, to combine concepts from all three theories. Moreover, the combination of the three theories meets the needs of younger leaders who manage older leaders and it also meets the needs of experienced leaders who are influenced by other leaders in a higher position of authority. The younger leaders need mentoring to develop their management and leadership skills, and the experienced leaders need mentoring-type behaviors from superior leaders to serve in authenticity without the usurping of their authority. The theoretical foundation and findings of my research study and other empirical studies will be shared in greater detail in a future book publication. This book, however, will focus on the biblical foundation of mentor-based leadership.

The five elements of Bloom Leadership encompass concepts from these three leadership theories as well as reconceptualized concepts that are tailored to more contemporary organizational environments. Moreover, the elements resemble a mentoring style of leadership that is based on respect and a desire to see others flourish. This mentor-based style was used by Jesus and others in the Bible who were effective in training and preparing people to serve at a higher level. Let us examine these biblical examples more closely.

Remember from the Preface that the term *leader* is used to describe someone who is in a higher position of authority or an individual who influences and inspires others towards the vision of an organization. In addition, the term *follower* is used to describe an individual who is in a lower position or who desires to be influenced by a leader for the purpose of development. It is important to note that a follower can also be a leader who is influenced by another leader in a higher position of authority. This 'leaders leading leaders' concept will be explored more in Chapter 3.

Element 1 – Acceptance

Leader/Follower Example
Jesus/Samaritan Woman

Scripture Reference(s)
John 4:30, 39-42
(God offers living water to all who long for acceptance)

Overview – Acceptance

The pain of rejection, especially if it comes from those closest to you, can stay with you for a lifetime. Your reality and how you see other people are affected, and you may end up feeling inferior and unworthy of love and respect. On the one hand, you long for acceptance, but on the other, you keep your distance from people out of concern that you will be rejected again.

This was the back story of the woman who Jesus met at the well in the village of Sychar in Samaria. It was noon. Why would anyone go out to get water in the noonday heat unless they didn't want to be around people? We also learn in the conversation that she'd had five husbands and the one she was currently living with was not her husband. Her rejection stood out immediately. When Jesus asked for a drink of water, she replied, *"You are a Jew, and I am a Samaritan woman. Why are you asking me for a drink?"* (John 4:9) In other words, she was saying, "We have nothing to do with one another." Of course, Jews were not encouraged to communicate with Samaritans, but her words were laced with bitterness. Jesus could see through her roughness into her loneliness and her longing for acceptance; but, more than that, He saw her spiritual dryness and thirst. And so, He offered her His living water. *"Anyone who drinks this water will soon become thirsty again. But those who drink the water I give will never be thirsty again. It becomes a fresh, bubbling spring within them, giving them eternal life"* (John 4:13-14).

The woman immediately asked for this water so that she would never have to come the well again for water – the living water. This translates into, "I want this living water so that I will never have to experience rejection and loneliness again. I want this living water so that I will never have to give up and hide because of disappointment and failure in my relationships. I want this living water so that I can learn to love and trust again."

Acceptance was the door to the woman's heart. Acceptance is crucial for our wholeness and self-esteem. Acceptance is *welcoming, receiving*, and *affirming*. According to the Oxford English Dictionary, the definition for acceptance is *the action or the process of being received as adequate or suitable, recognizing the other person for who he or she is, and being attentive to the circumstances of the relationship moment by moment.*

When your new life in Christ begins, there are essential guidelines to follow in the relationship. Leaders should accept a follower or a mentee who has been assigned or chosen to work with them and be committed to the growth and development of others. It is important to nurture those mentoring relationships. In the same way, it is beneficial to accept followers or mentees with their vulnerabilities. What does it *mean* to accept someone with their vulnerabilities? Previously, we defined acceptance as *welcoming, receiving*, and *affirming*. It means you're not shrugging a person off because of appearance or other unacceptable reasons. You give them the opportunity of acceptance because God first accepted us without reservation when we came to Him. It is important to note that followers have as much responsibility in the mentoring relationship as the leaders do. Leaders can guide and teach to the best of their ability, but followers must be willing to grow and develop or it will never happen.

God also gives us a beautiful illustration of acceptance in how He handles His relationship with us. He is loving, welcoming, and desires to receive others unconditionally. While He corrects and convicts, He is never judgmental. When He shows you the problem, He always gives you the solution. In turn, we must be humble, willing to change, and aware that we need help. We must also accept the grace to change that God so freely offers. This is an example of what a healthy relationship with God looks like from both sides, with God as the leader who accepts those who also accept Him.

Leader Responsibility

Who we are in Christ both as a believer and as a leader transcends race or culture or religion. When the woman said that Jews worship in Jerusalem, whereas Samaritans worship on Mount Gerizim, she was talking about race, culture, and religion. Jesus countered her divisive remark by being all-inclusive, "*But the time is coming—indeed it's here now—when true worshipers will worship the Father in spirit and in truth. The Father is looking for those who will worship him that way*" (John 4:23). God accepts ALL who would come to Him in faith believing that Jesus Christ is Lord. We come, not on our own merits, but through the blood of Jesus who ransomed us from the enemy. We are accepted no matter how messed up we think we are.

Just as God made salvation and everlasting life available to all, your role as a leader requires you to never exclude anyone assigned to you from your mission. We must do this if we truly desire to honor Him in our organizations. Anything less would put us in opposition to the type of people God has called us to be. If we are to take after Jesus in our role, we must likewise be willing to accept everyone for who they are, even before they bloom into their full potential. Moreover, we must be willing to look past their weaknesses and see their innate potential already fulfilled. Prayerfully, they will receive your developing and respond appropriately.

Follower Responsibility

As soon as the Samaritan woman's eyes were opened to see that Jesus was indeed the Messiah, she wanted His living water. What's more, she didn't just keep the good news to herself. She ran back to the village (forgetting her natural water and water bucket), spreading the message to the people. She was now making an effort to interact with the very people she had previously avoided. You see, the living water bubbles inside of you and must flow out to others. Rather than feeling ostracized, she was now willing to be heard – for she had something to say, and she knew how to say it because of her encounter with Jesus. She was so effective that the people ran to the well to see Jesus for themselves and, when they heard Him preach in their village, they also believed and were saved. This rejected woman who received acceptance now becomes an ambassador for the Kingdom! Although this is not expressly stated in the Bible account, we can safely assume that her salvation and that of the whole village would be the beginning of a transformation because what God sets out to do, He will accomplish.

Action/Application

Jesus accepted the Samaritan woman by not condemning her and making living water available to her. As a leader, do you take time during the day to greet people at various levels and determine if you have what they need to thrive within the organization? The Samaritan woman accepted salvation in return. Acceptance is a two-way street, and when followers are eager to participate in the opportunity presented to them, people outside of the leadership relationship may benefit as well. In this case, the Samaritan woman preached about Jesus to the entire village, so they also benefited from her encounter with Jesus. When acceptance is a priority, people within the organization will be more determined, more committed, and more equipped to help carry out and achieve the mission. Followers should be teachable at all times. Leaders must be compassionate and willing to look beyond themselves into the heart and lives of others. It is critical for both the leader and the follower to remember the benefits of the relationship they have chosen to accept throughout the process.

"Make every interaction count...even the small ones. They are all relevant."

– Shep Hyken

Element 2 – Appreciation

Leader/Follower Example
Paul/Church at Philippi

Scripture Reference(s)
Philippians 1 – 4
(Paul's letter to the Philippians)

Overview – Appreciation

    The second element in Bloom Leadership is appreciation. Appreciation can be expressed through *motivation* and/or *rewards*. As leaders, we should show appreciation for the efforts of others publicly or privately in the form of verbal praise or tangible incentives for their efforts. Some people do not need the money or even a gift card. Instead, they appreciate simple things like saying, "Thank you." Whether it is a simple gesture or a substantial reward, the important thing is that it makes others feel appreciated, worthy, and encouraged. It boosts their self-esteem, strengthens their relationship with you and renews their dedication to the organization.

    The biblical account of how Paul showed his appreciation to the church in Philippi speaks volumes about how we can express our gratitude to followers in order to strengthen them. Paul was specially commissioned by the Holy Spirit to go to Macedonia to preach the gospel, and Philippi was the first church he planted there – in fact, it was the first church in Europe (See Acts 16:6-8). Paul had met Lydia, a trader of purple dye, in the city and led her to Jesus. From there the home group she led blossomed into a church.

It was at Philippi, too, that Paul and Silas ministered to the jail keeper and family who very likely became members of the church (See Acts 16:25-40). Both the divine calling and the close personal ties brought Paul into a very special relationship with the Philippians as reflected in the opening salutation of his letter, "*I thank my God upon every remembrance of you, always in every prayer of mine making request for you all with joy, for your fellowship in the gospel from the first day until now…*" (Philippians 1:3-5 NKJV). In this opening, Paul talks about remembering them, his constant prayer for them, the joy they brought him and their partnership with him in the gospel. He ends the letter by calling them "*my beloved and longed-for brethren, my joy and crown…*" (Philippians 4:1 NKJV). These kind words went beyond the usual greetings because they showed a very close bond and were made even more meaningful by the dire situation. First of all, Paul was writing while he was imprisoned in a Roman cell, where he felt he would not survive. In the midst of all that pain, he made it a point to write to them to show his love and appreciation for them, dispatching one of their members Epaphroditus with that letter.

One of the main reasons for Paul's deep affection was the Philippians' eagerness to work with him for the furtherance of the gospel (verse 5), a partnership that involved prayer and sharing the truth of Christ in word and in action (verses 27-28). They also suffered for their faith alongside Paul (verses 29-30), which involved persecution from the outside, confronting heresies, and their own internal conflicts. And, of course, we cannot forget the Philippians' financial support of Paul's ministry. This particularly touched him, knowing their own dire need.

> *Now you Philippians know also that in the beginning of the gospel, when I departed from Macedonia, no church shared with me concerning giving and receiving but you only. For even in Thessalonica you sent aid once and again for my necessities. Not that I seek the gift, but I seek the fruit that abounds to your account. Indeed I have all and abound. I am full, having received from Epaphroditus the things sent from you, a sweet-smelling aroma, an acceptable sacrifice, well pleasing to God* (Philippians 4:15-18 NKJV).

Leader Responsibility

How could Paul repay such faithful people from his prison cell? This is what he says about their support: *"Not that I seek the gift, but I seek the fruit that abounds to your account"* (Philippians 4:17). In other words, he is earnestly praying that every spiritual blessing in the heavenly places be showered upon them, including material blessing, peace, joy, and empowerment. Paul was also sending Epaphroditus and Timothy to encourage and build them up.

The Philippians would be deeply touched in knowing that he truly appreciated them. No matter the trials he was going through, Paul's thoughts were constantly turning towards those to whom he owed such a debt to in terms of prayer, ministry, and financial and moral support. Finally, he released a powerful impartation so that they, too, might know the depths of Christ *"and the power of His resurrection, and the fellowship of His sufferings, being conformed to His death."* In this, Paul commended them for being counted worthy of suffering for Christ. *"For to you it has been granted on behalf of Christ, not only to believe in Him, but also to suffer for His sake, having the same conflict which you saw in me and now hear is in me"* (Philippians 1:29-30, emphasis added).

As we show those following us not only our appreciation and love but also the challenges we are going through, we are lifting them up and strengthening their resolve to be like-minded, courageous, and full of faith.

Follower Responsibility

The Philippians would undoubtedly respond to the letter with relief upon learning that Paul was still alive. They would be appreciative of him pouring out his soul to them and they would respond to his command to be like-minded with hope, joy, and faith. Additionally, they would continue the mission regardless of what happened to Paul.

Therefore if there is any consolation in Christ, if any comfort of love, if any fellowship of the Spirit, if any affection and mercy, fulfill my joy by being like-minded, having the same love, being of one accord, of one mind (Philippians 2:1-2).

Action/Application

If this were the last letter from someone you cherished, every word of theirs would be taken and applied very seriously. The words of that person would live on. Down the road, century after century those same words would carry the same weight to believers who would find them a source of great strength and joy in all their tribulations. There are so many rich and wonderful truths to teach us about standing firm in our Christian faith, persevering through challenges, and most importantly, helping others to persevere as well – all glory to God!

In the work setting, appreciation is a reciprocal exchange between both giver and receiver. In an atmosphere of expressing gratitude, praise, and reward, there will be a corresponding response to receiving that commendation and trying to excel not only to meet objectives but to firm up human relationships. Expressing appreciation reduces tension and conflict and makes the environment so much more conducive to good interpersonal relations and more productive work. Therefore, as leaders, consider showing appreciation to others in word or in deed.

"Clearly, there aren't enough positive moments or interactions happening in the workplace. As a result, our economy suffers, companies suffer, and individual relationships suffer."

– Tom Rath

Element 3 – Admiration (Respect)

Leader/Follower Example
Naomi/Ruth

Scripture Reference(s)
Ruth 1 – 4
(Naomi and Ruth's journey to a better life)

Overview – Admiration (Respect)

    Bloom Leadership defines admiration as *respect, esteem, reverence, honor*, and *warm approval* for someone else. The story of Naomi and Ruth provide an excellent example of consideration and respect between a leader and a follower. There was a great famine in Israel during the time when the judges ruled, and many people migrated to foreign lands to find food for their families. A man from Bethlehem named Elimelech left with his wife Naomi and his two sons Mahlon and Kilion to find a new life in Moab. Elimelech died and Naomi continued to live with her two sons who married Moabite women named Orpah and Ruth. Both sons also passed away leaving Naomi with her two foreign daughters-in-law. When Naomi got word that the famine in her land was over, she decided to go back to Bethlehem. She suggested that Orpah and Ruth stay in Moab where they had a better chance of finding new husbands. While Orpah returned to her mother's home, Ruth clung to Naomi and told her:

BLOOM

Entreat me not to leave you, Or to turn back from following after you; For wherever you go, I will go; And wherever you lodge, I will lodge; Your people shall be my people, And your God, my God (Ruth 1:16).

Naomi cared for Ruth with all of her heart, and she desired the best for Ruth, even at her own expense. Upon their arrival in Bethlehem, Naomi instructed Ruth to go into the barley field to glean the leftover grain. She worked behind the harvesters in a field that belonged to a man named Boaz, who was a relative of her father-in-law. When Boaz heard that Naomi had returned with Ruth and that Ruth was gleaning the leftover grain, he assured her of her safety while working in his fields. Boaz had heard of Ruth's kindness toward Naomi and was touched by it.

Ruth worked very hard in the fields to provide enough barley to sell and to keep for her and Naomi. After the harvest, Naomi encouraged Ruth to meet Boaz on the threshing floor and to lie down at his feet when he was sleeping. Ruth followed her instructions exactly. She took a bath and put on fragrance to look pleasing and appealing to Boaz. Boaz gave Ruth six measures of barley for her to take home to Naomi. Later, Boaz marries Ruth with the blessing of the entire community, and Ruth is accepted within their culture.

Naomi expressed genuine concern for Ruth by initially requesting that she remain in Moab so that she could have a better chance of remarrying within her own culture. Naomi did not make the decision for Ruth to follow her to Bethlehem. Instead, she suggested what she thought was best for Ruth, and allowed her to make the decision out of respect. When Ruth, of her own free-will, chose to follow her mother-in-law and accept her Jewish faith and culture, she was honoring Naomi by putting complete trust in her. All of Naomi's actions in their story were done to lead Ruth to growth in her life.

Leader Responsibility

Leaders should provide guidance and advice to followers by offering suggestions as necessary. Instead of compelling Ruth to travel to Bethlehem, Naomi suggested that she stay in Moab, allowing Ruth to make the ultimate decision regarding her growth. Furthermore, leaders should not command action from followers, but they should inspire and encourage them to reach higher goals. Naomi was an amazing illustration of what it means for leaders to invest in others. She spent time with Ruth, teaching her how to win the heart of Boaz, which proved to be beneficial to both of them. Naomi was able to excel in leadership because she admired Ruth, and, in turn, Ruth was willing to be led.

Follower Responsibility

Ruth was a phenomenal follower in that she desired to be influenced by Naomi's leadership, and she valued the respect and honor Naomi showed her by responding in kind. She also put aside Naomi's practical advice to remain in Moab because she recognized her higher calling of remaining with Naomi – to be tutored about her faith and culture. Ruth was thankful for Naomi's guidance, showing dedication and gratitude every step of the way.

Additionally, Ruth's willingness to respectfully follow Naomi's instructions concerning Boaz helped her to win his heart and eventually marry him. Ruth showed Naomi honor by working side-by-side with her as she knew that her growth would be multiplied by the time spent learning from Naomi. Similarly, followers should desire to spend time and work as a team with leaders to accomplish goals. To add to that, followers should be willing, as Ruth was, to be trained by wise leaders once a commitment is made to be mentored.

Action/Application

This story of Naomi and Ruth is a fantastic example of a healthy leader/follower dynamic. In a business setting, are you willing to respect and esteem those who follow you? Do you demonstrate your concern for others? Do you provide advice and guidance when it comes to meeting goals and objectives? As a leader, you should be genuinely concerned for those who join you in carrying out the organization's mission. You should also provide support where possible and contribute to the development and growth of others. Respect and honor, which are key components of admiration, involve allowing others to be authentic and to make decisions concerning their growth. Sometimes followers will concur with the recommendations made by leaders, being completely willing to carry out the directives that have been given. And at other times, they desire a different path. Either way, mutual respect will help to maintain the honor and trust the relationship needs to thrive.

"If toxic behavior in a workplace is left unchecked, it will spread and kill the organization. The only antidote is strong, positive leadership. Be a leader."

– The Leadership Reformation

Element 4 – Advisement

Leader/Follower Example
Paul/Timothy

Scripture Reference(s)
Acts 16:1-3
(Paul met Timothy)

1 Timothy 1:1-4
(Paul called Timothy a true son in the faith)

Overview – Advisement

Bloom Leadership defines advisement as *guidance, careful consideration, advice, or counsel*. This element is all about providing coaching and mentoring with the expectation of growth or progress. We are going to examine the relationship between Paul and Timothy when discussing this element. Their relationship is perhaps one of the most relevant biblical examples of advisement and how we can apply it to our leadership.

Timothy was from the Lycaonian city of Lystra in Asia Minor. Because he was born of a believing Jewish mother and a Greek father, Timothy became a Christian believer. According to Acts 16:1-3, Paul met Timothy on his second missionary journey, and he became Paul's disciple and co-worker along with Silas. Paul worked with Timothy in establishing churches at Philippi, Thessalonica, and Berea (See Acts 16:1-17).

The relationship of Paul and Timothy is such an outstanding biblical example of advisement because their working dynamic brought the gospel message to all the regions they visited. This contributed to the spread of Christianity in the Mediterranean region of the world. The teamwork they demonstrated fueled their mission. Paul effectively coached and mentored Timothy. Then, when Timothy was ready, Paul gave him many opportunities to go and practice what he had learned. We are blessed to have their story documented so that we can emulate it in our own organizations.

When Paul couldn't go to certain places, he sent Timothy on his behalf. Before Paul sent Timothy to a place to minister, he sent word before Timothy even got there – words endorsing Timothy's leadership and showing confidence and trust in him to carry out the assignment. That's what leaders should do: coach, mentor, encourage, endorse, and invest time in their mentees. They should also give mentees an opportunity to carry out those things they have been taught.

Leader Responsibility

Paul was so intentional about Timothy's growth that he considered him a son. He spoke highly of Timothy, recognizing his potential. Paul encouraged Timothy and gave him opportunities to utilize his abilities by visiting other churches and ministering there. This delegation served to spur Timothy on to new growth. In these new places, Timothy was able to apply the wisdom passed on to him by Paul. In all this, he allowed Timothy to move from son to co-laborer, from being his follower to being a greater leader himself. Lastly, Paul worked alongside Timothy and invested in him along the way.

Follower Responsibility

Timothy had a genuine desire to grow even though he was already a leader when he met Paul. He assisted Paul in establishing churches in the region and was obedient to Paul's guidance. He accepted redirection and was willing to do whatever it took for the mission. The calling on his life from God and confirmation by Paul motivated him to see the missions through to fruition.

Action/Application

Leaders who make a commitment to mentor others should be willing to guide, correct, counsel, teach, and be patient in their interactions. Just as important, followers must also be teachable, coachable, open to feedback, willing to learn, and humble. This kind of reciprocal sharing and receiving of wisdom will ultimately boost productivity and satisfaction within the organization.

The following chapter delves deeper into Paul and Timothy's mentoring relationship, focusing on how leaders influence or mentor others who also serve in leadership roles.

The interactions between leaders and followers impact the culture and success of an organization. To change the culture, management must teach and expect individuals within the organization to improve their interactions.
– C. D. Dudley

Element 5 – Advancement

Leader/Follower Example
Moses/Joshua

Scripture Reference(s)
Numbers 20:9-12
(Moses smote the rock in disobedience)

Numbers 27:17-23
(Moses laid his hands upon Joshua in obedience)

Overview – Advancement

Bloom Leadership considers advancement as *the process of promoting the development, improvement, growth, or furtherance of someone.* Oftentimes, people think of advancement only as climbing the ladder or getting promoted, but advancement also includes training, empowerment, exposure, challenging assignments, and skills development. Jesus' leadership with the disciples is our prime and ultimate example of this as He demonstrated the characteristics that make a leader successful and create powerful followers.

One of the greatest strengths of mentoring leaders is the ability to reproduce others who can carry out the work that you've done. To do so, you must teach, by word and by action, those who are under your auspices. Jesus effectively taught large groups and the people marveled at the wisdom and authority of His words. But He was also heavily involved in teaching small groups of disciples and followers who were made up of ordinary lay people – not religious people. They were diverse and anything but perfect.

BLOOM

In order to advance, you have to acquire knowledge and skills, maybe even seek further education. Some people gain knowledge and skills on their own, but others select a mentor who is already in a position similar to the one that they desire. Some are mentored even by their supervisors or another person at a higher level within or outside the organization. It is also possible to acquire the necessary skills through experience. Whatever the case, when you're wanting to advance, you have to acquire the required skill sets. So, as a leader, you should be willing to allow those who are under your charge to be trained and empowered to develop their skills. Have you ever worked with someone who refused to allow you to receive training? Have you ever worked for someone who always wanted to go themselves but never allowed you to go even though you had the capacity to excel? Imagine, for a moment, how someone would feel if you, as a leader, treated them in this very stifling way.

I have found that disapproval of training often happens when a leader is insecure about their position. They may be afraid that they will be out of a job if others are allowed to share their knowledge and skills. But, as a leader, you should be confident in your abilities and look to train people to assist you in your efforts or replace you at some point. It is essential to build up successors to whom you're willing to pass on your knowledge and skills. Are you also at that place where you have developed, and now it's time for you to help develop others? Are you willing to pass on what you know?

Let's look at what we can learn from Moses' "retirement" and the appointment of Moses' successor, Joshua. At the end of the children of Israel's wanderings in the wilderness for forty years, it was time to enter the Promised Land. Would Moses be the one to lead the people? No. Moses would not be commissioned to lead the people, neither would he be allowed to go across. Like the entire generation who had believed the negative report of the ten spies (See Numbers 13 and 14) and had died in the wilderness, Moses would die without walking into the Promised Land.

Joshua was not at fault for Moses' inability to cross over Jordan into the land that God promised. Moses had disqualified himself because he had dishonored the LORD's command to speak to the rock at Meribah to get water. Instead of simply speaking to the rock as God instructed, he struck it twice in his anger at the people. The LORD said, *"Because you did not trust in me enough to honor me as holy in the sight of the Israelites, you will not bring this community into the land I give them"* (Numbers 20:12).

BLOOM LEADERSHIP

Then Moses earnestly asked the LORD to appoint a successor so that the congregation of the LORD would not be *"as sheep with no shepherd"* (Numbers 27:17). The LORD's choice was Joshua:

Take thee Joshua the son of Nun, a man in whom is the spirit, and lay thine hand upon him; And set him before Eleazar the priest, and before all the congregation; and give him a charge in their sight. And thou shalt put some of thine honour upon him, that all the congregation of the children of Israel may be obedient. And he shall stand before Eleazar the priest, who shall ask counsel for him after the judgment of Urim before the LORD: at his word shall they go out, and at his word they shall come in, both he, and all the children of Israel with him, even all the congregation.

And Moses did as the LORD commanded him: and he took Joshua, and set him before Eleazar the, and before all the congregation:

And he laid his hands upon him, and gave him a charge, as the LORD commanded by the hand of Moses (Numbers 27:18-23).

Why did the LORD choose Joshua over Moses' sons, or Eleazar the priest, or Caleb the other spy who sided with Joshua? There were three qualities that stood out in Joshua over and above the others:

- **Intimacy with the LORD and full of His spirit.** Exodus 33:11b tells us that "*Joshua, son of Nun, did not leave the tent.*" During the wilderness days Joshua was constantly in communion with God at the tabernacle of meeting. His ability to hear from the Lord would be critical in the battles that lay ahead.
- **Close relationship with Moses.** Joshua had been Moses' minister from his youth (See Numbers 11:28). Working closely with Moses, he waged battles against the Amalekites and other enemies, witnessed the crossing of the Red Sea, and saw many signs and wonders. Joshua was recognized, unofficially, as a leader who was influenced by Moses and as a leader who influenced others.
- **Boldness and courage.** It was Joshua and Caleb who gave a good report of the Promised Land, urging the people to go up and take the land contrary to the negative report of the ten spies (See

Numbers 14:7-9). Boldness and courage were needed to stand against the pressure of the people and to lead with radical faith.

Although Caleb was equally courageous, Joshua was already the favored assistant of Moses and had fought closely beside him as a warrior. Moses and Joshua had mutual respect for one another as worked together. Leadership continuity was critical because, just as the people had accepted Moses, they had to accept his designated successor.

When Joshua assumed leadership, he reinstated this continuity by reaffirming the promise given to Moses to go into the land, *"which the* LORD *your God giveth you to possess…Remember the word which Moses the servant of the* LORD *commanded you, saying, The* LORD *your God hath given you rest, and hath given you this land"* (Joshua 1:1,13). The people wholeheartedly accepted his leadership and promised to do as he instructed (See Joshua 1:16-18).

Leader Responsibility

Moses already had confidence in Joshua when he sent him out with the others to spy out the land of Canaan (See Numbers 13). Joshua passed the leadership test by showing his faith and courage in spite of the odds. During the wilderness experience, Moses began to give Joshua more opportunities to serve. Two notable examples of Moses' trust in Joshua as his assistant are seen here:

- When Moses went up to the mountain to be with the LORD, he took Joshua with him, while he told the elders to wait below. *"And Moses rose up, and his minister Joshua: and Moses went up into the mount of God"* (Exodus 24:13). This is amazing because we know that whoever touched the mountain would be put to death (See Exodus 19:12). But Moses recognized that Joshua was a man who could be trusted with sacred things because he was close to the LORD and his heart was right with the LORD.

- In a major engagement with the Amalekites at Rephidim, Moses appointed Joshua as leader in the battle. Moses himself stood at the top of the hill raising his hands in prayer. As long as Moses held up his hands, the Israelites were winning, but whenever he lowered his hands, the Amalekites won. So, when Moses' hands grew tired, Aaron and Hur held each of his hands up on either side so his hands remained steady till sunset. In this way, Joshua overcame the Amalekite army. Joshua on the ground was physically engaged with the enemy, while the intercessor Moses and his assistants fought against the forces of darkness in the spirit realm (See Exodus 17). This battle plan would show to Joshua the dynamics of fighting the LORD's battles the LORD's way and the necessity for all parties to be of one heart, one mind, trusting in their God and one another.

Joshua was given many more opportunities to learn and develop as a leader because he had proven himself at this battle. Although Moses did not officially appoint him second in command, it was in a position of service alongside Moses that he was able to be trained in military and spiritual warfare.

Follower Responsibility

Joshua responded favorably to Moses' training and the opportunities to prove his bravery by honoring and obeying his commands. This was the essence of his role as a follower because he always supported and never challenged his leader. In this way, he earned his leader's trust, enough to allow him to engage in a major battle.

This principle is so important to understand because Moses made several mistakes along the way. One was perhaps not being assertive enough when the people were ready to side with the negative report of the ten spies. Moses could have rebuked them and stood with Joshua and Caleb. Rather, there is no record of him making a pronouncement, and there is no record of any protest from Joshua either. Joshua respected his leader's silence. Neither was he critical when Moses smote the rock in anger. No, he was always behind the scenes, learning, assisting, and leading when asked. Joshua was given many opportunities to be trained and empowered to carry out major responsibilities under Moses' leadership. The people learned obedience and respect for their leader, Moses, no doubt encouraged by Joshua's influencer role.

Action/Application

Good leaders and followers must surrender their own personal ambitions to the vision and mission of the organization. They see their role as supporting its values and the objectives that must be accomplished at each stage. They must know when there is a change of course. Leaders train, mentor, and coach followers through formal and hands-on experiences, constantly challenging them with novel tasks. Even though followers are exposed to risk, good leaders are present to support them and protect them. Good leaders are also secure in their calling and do not feel threatened by the talents of followers. Instead, leaders give them the space to develop. When good leaders see followers rise in an authority of their own, these leaders are ready to prepare followers to be their successors or be promoted in some other capacity.

Good followers learn from observing leaders through both the strengths displayed as well as their weaknesses. They never maliciously expose the weaknesses of the leader which would weaken the enterprise. Instead, they are always available to patiently serve, as Joshua did for Moses.

Sometimes, we find followers in organizations that simply do not wish to change and learn something new. This refusal of growth limits them, holds them back from being all they can be, and it slows down the mission of the entire organization. We must always remember the vital responsibility that followers share as well. Every developmental relationship is a two-way street, and the process of advancement is no exception.

The five elements discussed in this chapter do not cover all of the functions or behaviors that leaders should adopt to assist others in their quest for development, but they are a good place to start and will boost productivity, morale, and satisfaction in the process.

THREE

LEADERS LEADING LEADERS

BLOOM

While most of the time, we associate leadership with the relationship between leaders and followers, it can also exist between a leader and a follower who also happens to be a leader (middle manager, supervisor, subordinate leader, etc.). In the latter situation, a connection or relationship exists between two individuals who are both visionaries and responsible for their respective areas of responsibility. In my discussion of leaders leading leaders, **I am primarily referencing** two people who are in a position of authority and are responsible for the management or development of others in some way. This use of the word "leader" is more formal, and it does not simply refer to a person's level of influence. In my discussion of the elements of Bloom Leadership, having vision and being accountable separate leaders from followers, even though I believe that everyone is a leader in some capacity. Although some followers may be highly influential or lead, they may not have the power to set the team's vision, make final decisions, or take full responsibility for team actions. In light of this, it's crucial to comprehend that the idea of "leaders leading leaders" refers to two leaders who have both authority and influence.

In this chapter, I provide a more detailed explanation of the dynamic of leaders leading leaders – where you have one leader who is in a position of authority being led or influenced by another person in a position of higher authority. When a leader who has reached a pinnacle of success and another leader on the cusp of success come together, both walking in respect and humility, then there is room for God to move mightily in the midst of the interaction. I'm convinced that this is how massive impact occurs within our ever-changing organizations.

As we return to the story of Paul and Timothy, there are a few more lessons that focus specifically on the aspect of leaders leading leaders. Even though both men were separated by distance at times, it is really incredible how dedicated Paul remained to his commitment to mentoring Timothy. Think about communication in those days – no email, no cell phones, and no social media. Regardless, Paul wrote to Timothy to encourage him in his new pastoral role. This kind of loyalty to his mentee was the result of being committed to God's calling on both of their lives. Do we follow our calling with the same passion?

Bloom Leadership defines blooming as *coming into full beauty or health*. Moreover, blooming encompasses flourishing, thriving, prospering, and progressing. This is exactly what Paul brought out in Timothy. Paul was a Bloom Leader because he was the catalyst that caused Timothy to bloom. He developed, equipped, and nurtured Timothy for a greater leadership role – the key word here is 'greater' because Timothy was already a leader when he met Paul. Even more crucial was the fact Paul carried out the process of developing Timothy following Scripture. In his first letter to Timothy, he continues his encouragement from afar: *"For physical training is of some value, but godliness has value for all things, holding promise for both the present life and the life to come"* (1 Timothy 4:8). Paul's style of leadership was transformational. He did more than train Timothy with physical preparation or training. He also nurtured Timothy's faith. That was key. Our roles do not only involve our physical selves, but our heart and soul as well. Here are some lessons from the Paul and Timothy's superior leader-subordinate leader dyad relationship.

Lead with a Parent-like Nature

In Paul's first letter to Timothy, he addresses him as *"my true son in the faith"* (1Timothy 1:2). In the corporate sense, see those you have committed to develop as mentees; in the ministry sphere, see them as sons and daughters. As you look at others in this way, you will start assuming a kind of parental responsibility for their growth. This responsibility comes from the Lord, and we must never take it for granted. God wants to do great work through the mentoring relationships that He has placed before us. When you interact in this way, it brings about some startling revelations. For instance, when our children mess up (which they most assuredly will), we may provide correction; but we do it out of love. We don't send them packing. They always have a place with us, and we continue being there for them. We desire that they do well and thrive in everything. It is the same with the people we lead. Even when they slip up in some areas, we are still there for them. We join with them in achieving their goals, and we cheer them on from the sidelines. Of course, there are cases where people are intentionally difficult or defiant, so the mentoring relationship may be more challenging.

> *...blooming encompasses flourishing, thriving, prospering, and progressing.*

One of my relatives likes to tell the story of her young daughter who was sitting in the backseat of the car one day and said, "Mommy, I want to be just like you when I grow up." My relative had inspired her daughter to desire to follow her example. That's what a leader does. That's what Paul did for Timothy.

He brought Timothy all the way from student, to son, to co-laborer. He invested the time and energy to see it through the entire way.

Although I have given my children a lot of coaching and guidance, I consider them to be leaders as well. Over the years, I have enjoyed collaborating with them on projects and events. And some of the knowledge and abilities they acquired while helping me with tasks have been put to use in college and in their careers. I trained them, and after some time, they were able to finish some tasks independently. I have to admit, that some of the tasks they completed independently were done better than I had taught them because of the technology they incorporated. Being mentored by their mommy was a blessing that helped them grow into the people God intended for them to be. Not only do I assist them, but they also assist me in a variety of ways. My oldest daughter is a master project coordinator who can take a large project and break it down into smaller pieces while incorporating the technology required to complete it flawlessly. My middle daughter observes what I do and say and gives me great feedback. By allowing her to contribute, I am honoring her and demonstrating that I value her contributions. It is beautiful to see the Holy Spirit working in your children as they grow in life, faith, and mission. Furthermore, it is so important that we partner with them to carry out tasks that will help them develop along the way. God has an incredible purpose for the lives of our sons and daughters – those we bore and those we have committed to developing. He has put us in the powerful role of having parental-type oversight in their journey.

Mentor Sons and Daughters

What is the value of being counted as a son or daughter? Imagine you are at home relaxing on your sofa, watching TV. Suddenly, one of the people you know from work comes to your house, without bothering to ring the doorbell. She goes into the kitchen, opens your refrigerator, and makes a sandwich. She also pours some juice and sits down on the sofa. Then, she takes your remote and starts channel surfing. Well, you are probably just sitting there thinking: "What just happened? Did I miss something?" Would you feel comfortable with coworkers, you barely know, doing that? Of course not! They do not have that type of authority or relationship with you.

Now, if your own son comes home from college and does the same thing, it is a little different. He walks in the door without knocking, goes into the kitchen, makes a sandwich, drinks some juice, and then sits down on the sofa and – apart from switching channels without your permission – his behavior is perfectly acceptable. He's your son; he has privileges in his own home. In the same way, we are sons and daughters of the Most High God – we have privileges because of our relationship. As a leader, you too will have people in your life who will have a special mentoring-type relationship with you, with more privileges because of your keen interest in their growth and development.

Can you see yourself treating those you mentor as beloved sons or daughters? Of course, you cannot mentor everyone like that and not everyone is entitled to such a close relationship with you. But the point is to build that relationship, build that trust, and see the results for yourself – more motivated and inspired people, ready and prepared to achieve success. For some, a transition to mentor takes place after they have acquired so much knowledge and insight. Just by reason of the overflow, they will have a desire to start pouring into other people. A way to ensure that all of your acquired wisdom and experiences live on beyond your years is by having mentees, or sons and daughters. This is one of the models of Bloom Leadership – pouring our knowledge into others to affect growth.

When you choose to be a mentor, the benefits are two-fold. The mentee is blessed because of the knowledge obtained and the privileges that come with the relationship. The mentor benefits by being able to disseminate knowledge and equip someone to help with and continue the mission of the organization. Again, you will not be able to personally mentor everyone, but you can treat everyone with mentoring-type behaviors that stem from respect. In any event, you must choose the right people to mentor – people who are willing to learn and grow through the process. There are so many things that you can share with them that they will not see in a textbook or self-help book. There may be some pitfalls they can avoid because of the spiritual wisdom you share. Imagine the great joy you would feel when someone succeeds in their role because you made time to develop a mentoring relationship with them and help set them up for greatness.

Be an Example of Excellent Leadership

In Paul's second letter to Timothy, he writes, "*You know what I teach, and how I love, and what my purpose in life is. You know my faith, my patience, my love, and my endurance*" (2 Timothy 3:10-11 NLT). How could Timothy have known all of those things about Paul if he hadn't spent time with him?

Paul showed Timothy all these things first-hand, by example. He spent time with Timothy, showing him how their mission was to be executed in practical ways on a day-to-day basis.

Because most people remember what they see more so than what they are told, it is important to model appropriate behavior and attitudes in front of them. Better yet, be the type of leader who models appropriate behavior whether someone else is watching. Don't run the risk of getting confused and forgetting to shift your behavior because someone else starts looking. Be consistent. Furthermore, resist being the type of leader who lectures about what should be done as opposed to showing others how to move forward by your example. Even after you have modeled the right type of behavior and attitude, go a step further and work with others to carry out tasks that you have shown them. Doing so will instill in them the importance of the task at hand and reinforce the training that you have provided or given them an opportunity to complete. It is important to understand that although you do a great job of exemplifying model behavior before others you mentor, they may carry out assignments differently at times or all of the time – and that's okay. Sometimes your influence has more to do with your character as opposed to how you go about getting certain things done.

Allow Others to Also Lead

The kind of training we provide or make available to others is crucial. As was already mentioned, mentees need mentoring and guidance, but letting them also learn through experience will help them develop the skills necessary for exponential growth. There is no substitute to this sort of training. A lecture or book, while perhaps imparting knowledge, will never replace what you gain from hands-on experience, while diving into the work. The next generation will benefit from our providing opportunities for them to "do" while being developed. It is absolutely crucial for them to obtain first-hand experience, or they will never truly be prepared to be a great leader themselves. Times have changed and our leadership styles should reflect the change that has occurred in our society as a result of advanced technology, quick access to information, and the increase in team-oriented environments. Change does not mean that we have to do away with our foundational teachings that keep us grounded and stable.

In his letter to the church in Rome, Paul writes, "*Timothy, my fellow worker, sends you his greetings*" (Romans 16:21). Paul's designation of Timothy as his fellow worker shows that he has graduated from a son or student to *co-laborer*. This didn't come about by merely listening to Paul's words, watching from the sidelines. Timothy rose to his newfound rank by working right alongside Paul in his mission and learning from Paul's direct example. Timothy was already a leader with his own vision. Not only do you need to be able to mentor people into leadership roles, it takes a special kind of grace to lead people who also have the authority to lead. You must trust them in their developed abilities and give them room to create and execute their own vision for the work ahead. As a leader who leads other leaders, we must emulate Paul's example with Timothy. We have to start seeing developing as DOING. It doesn't matter if it's 100%, 75%, 50%. Start the mentee off doing at least SOMETHING. You can add more to their plate once they are comfortable in their initial responsibilities. Through this model, Timothy went from son, to student, to co-laborer/colleague.

> *...it takes a special kind of grace to lead people who also have the authority to lead.*

Have you ever seen a plant that is crowded in its pot? It has a difficult time growing. Paul knew that Timothy was ready and wouldn't develop further, continuing as they were. He had full confidence in Timothy and sent him out into his very own ministry. He delegated to him and gave Timothy the opportunity to grow beyond the limitations of the pot he was in.

Paul set up Timothy for success and sent him on a mission. He helped pave the way for Timothy by announcing his arrival to the people of Corinth with his blessing:

For though ye have ten thousand instructors in Christ, yet have ye not many fathers: for in Christ Jesus I have begotten you through the gospel. Wherefore I beseech you, be ye followers of me. For this cause have I sent unto you Timotheus, who is my beloved son and faithful in the in the Lord..." (1 Corinthians 4:15-17)

Paul realized that it would take nothing from his power in preaching the Gospel to build up Timothy publicly. Because Paul spoke so highly of Timothy to the Corinthians, they wholeheartedly accepted Paul's nomination. This would go far in establishing Timothy's authority in Corinth. What did Paul say about

Timothy? He called him a "*son.*" He told the people of Corinth that Timothy was "*faithful.*" Those are some serious words, words that command power. Those are not words you just say about anyone!

    Just like Paul, once you have trained people who are for and with you, find the confidence in their abilities to delegate essential parts of your mission to them. Don't train them and then never trust them to carry out what they've learned. That's how we hold people down – by not allowing them to do anything. Additionally, don't be the type of leader who stands over others while they are doing their work, making them feel uncomfortable. And by all means, avoid unnecessarily criticizing them in public, causing them to be embarrassed, ashamed, and discouraged.

    You can't expect someone to grow when they are never given opportunities outside of their normal responsibilities or never go outside of their comfort zone. Is there a chance that they will fail? Yes, there is. But every failure is also an opportunity to grow. Oftentimes our greatest growth comes as a result of our greatest failure. Like everything else, mentorship is a journey of ups and downs, but the destination will still be the same. You trained them; now you must release them.

    Do you, as a leader, sometimes worry about who you send out because you do not know exactly what they are going to say or do? You may not trust them fully yet, but you know you have to send them out. The chance of success increases when people are exposed to what's appropriate. I am reminded of some of the things my mom used to say to us, as children, before we would go out somewhere. In essence, she was training us before we went out. She would say things like, "Now, when we go in here, you need to be on your best behavior. Don't touch anything that doesn't belong to you. Stay where I can see you, and don't embarrass me." That was the appropriate behavior in her eyes. Have you communicated what you deem acceptable or appropriate to those who you mentor or serve under your auspices? My mom took us with her for a while and spent countless hours letting us know what she expected. Then after we were older and she felt like we would behave properly, she gave us opportunities to go to the store in our neighborhood alone to get some of the things we needed. I cannot explain the excitement we felt having the liberty to go alone. We had grown to a place of trust and the experience of going all by ourselves increased our confidence. My mom didn't have to watch over us as much because she prepared us to be able to go out on our own. She benefited from our growth as we were able to help her with some of the necessary responsibilities.

LEADERS LEADING LEADERS

What I love about Paul is that it was easy for him to send Timothy. Paul had confidence that Timothy would model and communicate the proper things to the churches where he was sent. Paul also knew that he had fully equipped Timothy, and he respected his character. He had spent so much time with Timothy and invested in him to such a great degree that he knew he didn't have to worry about him. That's how you know that you did an excellent job with your mentee. Once you are established as a leader, remember that it takes nothing away from you to build up someone else. So, give people you mentor room to grow. Promote their development by endorsing them and honoring their close relationship to you. When you have somebody like Timothy whom you admire and develop, and who, in turn, is faithful, you know that you have done your job well. Moreover, you are blessed to have someone working with you who desires to learn from you – a person you may come to consider a son or daughter.

The relationship between Paul and Timothy is a beautiful example of how we are to treat others within our organization, including other leaders who also have vision or the potential to be greater visionaries. Be like Paul was to Timothy. Invest in the lives of up-and-coming leaders. Invest in their calling and give of your time and wisdom in order to see them thrive. Timothy was probably the biggest investment of Paul's time. Only one person, for sure, but how many did Timothy reach through the training and influence of Paul? Likewise, Jesus hand-picked only twelve, but the work that He did through them changed the world. Be assured that the time that you put into developing others will be multiplied in incredible ways for God's Kingdom.

Now that you've reviewed and comprehended the elements of Bloom Leadership, it's time for you to step up and initiate change within your organization. The next part of the book will provide key points on how to become a change agent and define your organization.

"There is almost no limit to the potential of an organization that recruits good people, raises them up as leaders and continually develops them."

– John Maxwell

PART II

Preparing for Change

FOUR

BECOMING A CHANGE AGENT

BLOOM

In the last section, you were provided with a description of "bloom" leadership as well as the five elements that it encompasses. This new type of leadership promotes a positive culture that improves satisfaction and productivity according to recent research studies. As mentioned previously, leadership is not only about leaders. Instead, it is about leaders and followers and how they interact across the organization to foster the type of positive culture that contributes to achieving goals and objectives. To this end, organizations should share their expectations about how individuals should interact. In this chapter, you will learn how culture impacts organizations, how to avoid gossiping, how to know your climate as a leader, and how to spark culture change.

Understanding the Impact of Culture

Organizational culture can be defined as a system of shared meaning. It is a set of unwritten norms that members of the organization accept and allow to guide their actions. Unfortunately, some prevalent workplace culture is that of clocking out the second it hits 5:00 pm, gossiping, treating others with disrespect, and just getting the bare minimum done and nothing more. This is the kind of culture that keeps us treading water and staying in the same place, not the kind that makes exceptional success happen, and certainly not the kind of culture that leads to new growth and people thriving. It is a culture that is very resistant to **change. However, the truth remains…change is necessary.**

The Lord is our ultimate example in everything, including the topic of culture and its impact. If we follow His lead and guidance, while letting Him shape our mission, there is nothing that can ultimately hold us back from our success. Remember God's promises, even when circumstances are difficult; as long as you follow His instructions, His promises will be fulfilled. If He has called you to something, and if you abide by His ways, He will surely give you "good success."

Not only must organizations define what they are and what they aspire to become, but they must also ensure that the culture is positive for maximum productivity and member satisfaction. The foundational aspect of creating a positive culture within your organization is changing your attitude about the people you are partnering with to achieve success. There is enough negativity that happens in any organization naturally. Sadly, it seems to be human nature to pick out the bad things in any given situation. You will always find people who take pleasure in backbiting and gossiping, which are two culture killers within ANY organization. They hinder your team's ability to be productive, which holds you back from success. Do you suspect that backbiting and gossip are going on within your organization? If so, start committing to a positive culture change.

Strategy and planning are important, but culture can have a more tremendous impact because your process won't work if the people in the organization don't know how to work cooperatively. Morale is crucial to motivating people to do their optimal work. Moreover, leaders should be committed to helping create an environment where people can perform. Someone who is not inspired, trained, and happy about what they are doing will not put their best foot forward. With culture being so critical, it is imperative to identify the types of cultural environment – positive, negative, and neutral. In doing so, we can learn to recognize the condition of the organization and create an action plan for culture change. This will help propel your mission to heights that it has never reached before, and this all starts with your leadership. Do not forget that you are the one who needs to drive change within your organization. Although it all begins with you, it does not end with you as everyone must be involved.

> *A positive culture is essential for an organization to accomplish its objectives and goals.*

Previously, I discussed in more detail, using Bloom Leadership elements, why it is important for both leaders and followers to understand their respective roles and how interacting more positively contributes to the organization's overall success. Thus, positive interactions become a serious focus of the Bloom Leadership.

Changing an organization's culture indeed is one of the most difficult leadership challenges that you may ever face. But does that mean that people have to be stuck in the culture they are in? Absolutely not! A positive culture is essential for an organization to accomplish its objectives and goals. I can assure you that cultural change is feasible. It takes a lot of planning, dedication, and hard work, but it is worth every effort.

Proverbs 29:18 is so important; let's look at it again, *"Where there is no vision, the people perish; but he who keepeth the law, happy is he."* When I read this verse, I think about the fact that thousands of organizations in the United States – corporate and religious – shut down every single year. Let that sink in. That is a vast and heartbreaking statistic. It is not just because of external forces, such as politics, government, or lack of demand. Many of the reasons these places have to close their doors forever are internal forces such as selfishness, lack of commitment, envy, and toxic relationships. All are elements of the organizational culture.

What we see all too often is that people just cannot get along with one another. The negativity that stems from relationships like this stifles the incredible results that come from people coming together with the unique strengths God has bestowed on them and doing something extraordinary *together*. If in the natural, such synergy can accomplish much, how much more can we do when we work together as the body of Christ! The absence or malfunctioning of any part of the body just slows down the whole operation and hurts everyone. This kind of negative culture stops us from accomplishing our goals together. That goes directly against why you accepted the role of a leader or started your organization in the first place. You started your journey as a leader to reach your goals.

Don't let a negative culture build up, while wreaking havoc on your success. Fight for what you created, and fight for what you believe in. But remember that our fight is not carnal; we fight with prayer, praise, and Christ-like strategy. The enemy attacks us the most fiercely when we are accomplishing something, so be prepared in every circumstance, armed with your faith, to retaliate and find victory in Christ. Sometimes it's easy to become so overwhelmed with the storms and the waves crashing in on us from all sides that it's hard to remember this truth. The enemy wants to deceive us into feeling like we are hopeless. But we are not!

To guide our ship in the right direction, we need the help of the people God has entrusted us with. He has put these people in our path for a reason. The unique gifts that He has given them will be crucial for our mission. We find our role in planning, organizing, leading, and communicating with these members to create the best team imaginable. To accomplish this, we need to set clear guidelines on what is expected regarding interactions and what roles people will play in the process. We also need to pray for others and help set them up for success, equipping them with the tools they need to achieve every one of their goals, while treating them respectfully as an instilled value.

BECOMING A CHANGE AGENT

It is therefore essential to seek the input from not only leaders, but followers as well. Everyone sees things from a perspective that is all their own, and we can learn much from considering other viewpoints. Thus, it is important to seek feedback and ideas from those in your organization. It not only helps them to feel like valued and important members of the team, but it opens up avenues to explore more possibilities. It offers you a fresh perspective on how you have been going about things and opens up potential opportunities to grow. Never forget the value of receiving feedback.

Know Your Climate

Not all leaders are the same. They use different styles and carry out different types of behaviors when influencing others to help meet organizational goals and building relationships. In other words, they have a certain climate which encompasses their style, personality, preferences, etc. Understanding your own climate and being willing to adjust when it interferes with your effectiveness as a leader are prerequisites for successfully developing others. If you don't understand your climate as a leader, pray and ask God, *"If any of you lack wisdom, let him ask of God, that giveth to all men liberally, and upbraideth not; and it shall be given him"* (James 1:5).

You can even take different types of assessments: personality, leadership style, leadership skills, and so on. If you fail to understand yourself and the environment, it will be difficult to help others working under your auspices thrive. The culture of the workplace goes a long way in determining the growth of the people within it. As expressed previously, if you want to change your organization's climate or culture, you must change the interactions. It needs to be clear that in every interaction, the organization's vision, mission, and core values are considered and there are expectations as to how people should treat each other.

There are three types of workplace relationships that take place within organizations: leader/leader, leader/follower, and follower/follower dyads. All of them require interactions. The more positive the interactions, the more positive the culture. The more positive the culture, the more satisfied the individuals in the organization. Studies show that the more satisfied people are in organizations, the more productive they are and the lower their intentions are to leave. Therefore, it is incumbent for leaders to work on improving interactions. This philosophy, as you may have determined, will be stressed over and over throughout this book.

The different types of people you meet or interact with can be compared to various plant vegetation. For example, cacti thrive in dry climates, while orchids thrive in a tropical rain forest. If you are the latter, and a cactus joins your organization, it is, more than likely, not going to be a place where they will reach their full potential. There is the possibility of adaptation to growing outside of their natural habitat to survive, but they will never become all they can be, and they will probably move on or continue to live without thriving or blooming. Then there are other plants like the Brazilian nut tree that will never adapt and cannot grow outside of its natural habitat as in some undisturbed jungles of the Amazon. Like that tree, some people will not be willing to adjust to your organization's climate or to your style of leading for various reasons, including their upbringing, their religious beliefs, their experiences, and even their personality. Their unwillingness to adapt to the culture of the organization is not a bad reflection on you; instead, they must find an organization that is a "good fit" for their development and future.

It is true that you should help others flourish as you strive for organizational success. Although investing all of this time is worth the effort, it is not without risk. You can experience crop failure. By that I mean, no matter how much time and energy you invest in someone, sometimes, it is just not going to work out for any number of reasons. It happens, and, again, it is okay. Be encouraged and keep moving.

The Emperor vs. the Gardener

The word *bloom* is in the title of this book because it is essential to our mission, which is to equip leaders with tools to utilize in their efforts to help others flourish and grow. To do this, a leader cannot be far removed from everything going on. Next, I will paint an illustration of poor leadership and an illustration of another leader who serves closely with people in the organization and meets their needs. The first illustration we will examine is that of an emperor.

The Emperor

Think back to what you may have learned about the times of the Roman colosseum games. This was a brutal competition where the Roman emperor sat up in the box, watching the gladiators thrash it out, and the winner was the last person standing. All the chaos is going on below, and the emperor is sitting in a high place watching. There was no leadership support and no teamwork involved. It was a fight to the death. This was a culture of pure chaos. The Roman officials who held these battles were unconcerned about the gladiators' well-being or growth; instead, they used them and the competition for their entertainment **and profitable gain.** You cannot be that kind of leader if you desire to influence actual culture change and not promote unhealthy and toxic competition. You have to be among the people sometimes, working on every level to build the best organization from the foundation up. Additionally, working at every level provides opportunities for you, as a leader, to identify individuals who you may want to personally mentor because of their potential to formally lead within the organization.

Have any of the environments you've been in felt like this at some point – a culture where chaos reigns and you feel left to fend for yourself? Have you ever worked for leaders who did not honestly care about your well-being or growth but were only interested in their gain by whatever means necessary? They watch from their high seat above and find amusement in the chaos below. That is not how productive organizations with a positive culture thrive and develop their talent. True leaders invest in the people and give of themselves to encourage the upward trajectory and growth of others. Furthermore, they take the time to personally mentor certain individuals, becoming intentionally committed to their success. Instead of feeling used by the organization, the individuals in a positive culture feel like a valued part of the mission they are striving to carry out. The task becomes their own, and not just that of the organization. They do not look up to see their leader looking down on them for sport, but instead, they see their leader side by side with them working on the mission together.

> *...if you want to change your organization's climate or culture, you must change the interactions.*

As shown in this illustration of toxic leadership, and what I like to call a chaotic culture, don't be an emperor-type leader. Cultivating a chaotic culture is not going to get leaders anywhere, even though there is a false sense of accomplishment because people are competing to win their attention, approval, or acceptance. Leaders will end up losing respect in the end, as well as hurting a lot of people along the way and stunting their growth. Some people even "die in discouragement," not wanting to ever try again or not giving their best when they are required to try again. Is this the type of leader you aspire to be? Of course, the answer should be unequivocally…no.

The Gardener

Let's look at another illustration, this time focusing on the type of leadership that drives culture change. This is the illustration of the gardener, who is committed to cultivating flowers in the garden and helping them to grow. Gardeners have a nature that is nurturing, full of kindness, and full of expectation. Picture in your mind what a gardener must do. The gardener has to get close to the flowers, pruning them, and speaking lovingly to them to nurture them. The flowers have to be 'pruned to bloom.' The leader that follows this illustration represents a good and healthy organizational culture. The gardener, unlike the emperor, is not sitting high above watching everything unfold. Instead, he is on his hands and knees in the garden, doing the hard work among the flower beds. He invests in the work, and it shows.

Moreover, a gardener helps different kinds of seeds to germinate in the right conditions. He will not expect cucumbers to grow from tomato seeds. When tomato seeds are planted in the ground, it would be wrong for the gardener to nurture them with the expectation of cucumbers. The gardener must know about the characteristics of the tomato seed and the optimum conditions for its growth because, again, all seeds are different.

How does a gardener help the seeds grow? He spends time: he prepares the ground, puts the seeds in the ground, waters the seed, and protects the seed. He starts by caring for the seed and then follows through with actions that demonstrate that care. Does the gardener just put the seeds in the ground and leave it at that? No, not at all. He watches over the seed's germination into seedlings and then blooming into full-grown plants ready for harvest. Now watch this: when the seed has fully grown and it is harvest time, seeds from that same harvest can be used to produce other seeds that will bring forth more flowers or vegetation. And then, where does the gardener help the seeds to grow? In the right environment. The seed must be placed in the type of soil that allows optimal growth. If the gardener does not have the right kind of soil or the proper items for care, then the seed may not survive.

It's the same way with a leader, who must be willing to spend time caring for the people he or she is nurturing. How does the leader help others to grow? One way is by using the five elements of Bloom

BECOMING A CHANGE AGENT

Leadership, accepting people for who they are. It's just like the tomato seed that this gardener is planting; he wants tomatoes to grow, and not cucumbers. When you're working with someone to develop them, you have to accept them for who they are and not who you want to force them to be. Yes, develop them…yes, help them to grow, but accept them for who they are.

I remember that my grandmother had a green thumb. She would be out in the garden early in the morning, just loving on her flowers. She would speak to her flowers, telling them how beautiful they were and encouraging them to grow. She truly cared for her flowers, putting in the hard work every day to watch them bloom. She was one of the inspirations for my leadership style. As she did with her flowers, I think it's extremely important that we put in the hard work necessary to encourage, support, and watch others bloom into everything they can be. When they bloom, they will bring joy to others that witness and behold their uniqueness…their awesomeness…their BLOOM. This is the attitude that we should have as leaders, one that is honed in on development and one that has an undying passion for engaging with other people.

> *Make every interaction meaningful and purposeful.*

Possess an attitude that encourages leaders to put in their best effort alongside everyone else, leading by example and enlightening them on what needs to be done. This creates a good and healthy culture so much needed in our organizations. A positive or nurturing culture does not come naturally – we must work hard to make it a reality. Understand that it is not always easy to maintain a positive culture, but just as the gardener has to prune the flowers for a lovelier bloom, it is necessary to help prune various attitudes and behaviors from time to time. But remember that everyone deserves to be treated with respect. Being respectful helps others receive and make the necessary corrections. At times, leaders may have to provide corrections so that others will be able to understand that there is a gap between current behavior and expected behavior.

The goal is to see the expected behavior that has been communicated. We see an example of this in the Bible when Jesus redirects Peter in Matthew 16:23, *"But when he had turned about and looked on his disciples, he rebuked Peter, saying, Get thee behind me, Satan: for thou savourest, not the things that be of God, but the things that be of men."* Jesus recognized that Peter had gotten off track in regard to the mission He had set forth for them, and He needed to take action to get Peter on the right path. We must do the same when people in our organizations are losing sight of the vision, mission, and the proper treatment of others. Jesus shows that it can be done. After Jesus ascended to heaven, Peter became the head of the Apostles and the early church. Moreover, Peter performed many miracles, preached powerful messages throughout various cities, and wrote two chapters of the Bible. As Christian leaders, we should be guided by our faith and by the established guidelines of our organizations when coaching others to change their behavior to meet desired expectations and enhance growth. Peter received correction from Jesus – his leader – and was better in the long run and not bitter. In the same way, when you have to correct others, ensure that they know that you care about them and their ability to carry out their assignment. In essence, you desire to see them "bloom."

Bruise and Bandage Mentality of Leaders

I used the descriptions of an emperor and a gardener in the previous section to illustrate examples of poor leadership and nurturing leadership. In this section, I want to explain two very harmful behaviors that leaders sometimes engage in and implore you to stay away from them because they affect culture negatively: gossiping and the "bruise and bandage" mentality. Both of these behaviors demonstrate a lack of respect for others. Understand that developing a team of individuals who are emotionally, spiritually, and physically prepared to move forward as they are inspired toward vision depends on having a culture that values respect.

Leaders who do not embrace the concept of mutual respect can leave people feeling hurt, disgusted, disappointed, resentful, embarrassed, ashamed, called out, disrespected, and discouraged. All of these feelings will suck the motivation right out of someone and not only leave them feeling unhappy with their work but also damage their self-esteem. Don't be the one who triggers such harm. The *bruise and bandage* mentality is where leaders try to tear someone down one minute, and then try to lift them back up the next minute – mainly because of guilt or remorse. In particular, leaders may chastise or "go off" on someone they manage or lead before they even have concrete proof or full details, only to later realize their error. Soon after, they return and try to make things right by giving the other person something that might make them feel better. Nevertheless, the damage has already been done. Trust in the leaders has diminished. The leader has damaged that relationship. Understand that fixing it after the fact is much more difficult than never causing the damage at all. Have you ever been treated in this manner by a leader, or have you ever acted in this manner toward someone else?

Even more damaging is when leaders hurt or disrespect others in public, unnecessarily. This brings humiliation and shame into the equation and further damages the honor and respect that leadership needs in order to thrive. Our words are powerful, and people do not easily forget when they are treated harshly, especially in front of their peers at work or others. If you are a leader, you should learn to focus more on developing individuals you are assigned to lead so that they will be in a better place to help you achieve the organization's mission and vision. Of course, this can prove to be quite a challenge sometimes.

I have had all types of leaders. The best leader I ever knew was a vice president who had a philosophy that was a game changer for me. He loved giving accolades to all the leaders who reported to him. When we did something great, he publicly acknowledged us, but when we fell short in some way, he did not embarrass us in public; instead, he coached us privately. He didn't chastise us publicly because he respected us as leaders. He also understood that we were responsible for the development and productivity of others who reported to us. Damaging us in public would erode their confidence in us and undermine our ability to influence others. In other words, he did not want to create an atmosphere of disrespect and dishonor, which would have made it more difficult for us to earn respect. So, he never shamed us publicly. Did we make some mistakes? You bet.

Another one of his maxims was, "If you're not making any mistakes, you aren't doing anything." Making honest mistakes is part of growth. It is a necessary part of our development. It is how to learn and become better. Great leaders, as he was, provide others with a "safe place to mess up" as development is taking place. As a result of his leadership style, we were able to set higher goals and take more risks, knowing that we had his support. The inspiration I garnered from my former supervisor's leadership has become so deeply embedded in me that it has formed the basis of much of my doctoral research and is the essence of this book.

The thing that I love about leading with respect is that you do not always have to quote scripture. You can live scripture. You do not always have to mention the Bible in people's faces, especially if you are in a corporate environment, but you can reflect Jesus, and so that is what my former boss did. I do not recall him quoting scripture in any meeting but by his actions, he showed he understood 1 Peter 2:17 that reads, *"Honour all men…"* He honored those who served under his wings. His most significant impact for me was in influencing my life and the lives of many other leaders so profoundly.

Gossiping Destroys Good Culture

I cannot discuss culture without sharing the negative effects of gossiping. Let me first define gossip, which is simply sharing information that should not be shared. Whether the gossip is true or false, it still damages morale and taints the overall atmosphere. This is one of the most significant issues that negatively affect the culture of an organization and causes toxicity and chaos. The Bible states, *"Let no corrupt communication proceed out of your mouth, but that which is good to the use of edifying, that it may minister grace unto the hearers"* (Ephesians 4:29).

To discern if what you are hearing is gossip or not, ask yourself this question: "If I am not the problem or the solution, why are they telling this to me?" If you cannot find the right answer to that question, what you are hearing is indeed gossip. In addition, there are three crucial questions to ask yourself to gauge if gossip is indeed a problem that can hinder interactions among stakeholders at your organization:

1. Do you think that gossiping/backbiting occurs within your organization?
2. Do you believe that gossiping/backbiting hinders your ability to be productive and successful as a team?
3. Would you like for gossiping/backbiting to stop?

Use those questions as a guide to develop a plan to eliminate gossip in your organization and create a healthy, positive culture that will make sure you carry out the mission and move closer to the vision of your organization. Furthermore, as a leader, consider having everyone participate in a "no gossiping pledge" for a certain number of days. The pledge can be completed electronically or using pen and paper. The act of making the commitment will start the shift in the atmosphere because people are intentional about using their words to be uplifting and encouraging.

BECOMING A CHANGE AGENT

Sparking Culture Change

In order to spark change in an organization's culture, leaders should foster an attitude of respect towards everybody while moving forward to accomplish organizational goals – this includes individuals at all levels and not just other leaders. The collective goal of every leader should be to develop, equip and nurture others to support the mission and vision of the organization. Bloom Leadership is about helping leaders lead others to develop and grow. Two fundamental questions to ask when assessing this goal are, "How am I developing them?" and "How am I equipping them?" This is true not only within your organizations but in your churches and households as well! We understand that leaders cannot make a commitment to personally mentor every person under his or her auspices. However, leaders can treat everyone with mentoring-type behaviors that stem from respect and result in increased satisfaction, productivity, and growth.

Other steps toward sparking culture change are clarifying expectations and rewarding accomplishments. How can you expect someone to do something if you don't tell them what you're expecting of them? It is simple: let people know what you expect them to do and reward or recognize them for doing it periodically. Some people are motivated by recognition and awards; they will strive to do what you say because of what they could possibly receive. Others have an internal motivation that drives them to work in excellence regardless of any type of appreciation that is shown. Therefore, knowing how others are motivated is important. Appreciation can come in the form of additional financial compensation or incentives, but make sure it is always coupled with personal recognition – private or public. Always let others know that they are valued and essential within the organization.

In addition to setting clear expectations, also be willing to help others set clear goals for growth. Partner with them in this and reward them for achieving those goals. Make sure that the goals are attainable, appropriate, measurable, and straightforward. These are critical. In your goal setting and providing clear expectations, it may be necessary for you to enforce your authority a bit. You don't have to flaunt it; you don't have to hold it over anyone's head, but you need to receive respect in your role and also give respect to others. Consider reminding those who work under your auspices that you are there to partner with them and help them develop in their respective roles and prepare for the future.

BLOOM

We can learn to be a mentoring leader by Paul's example in 1 Corinthians 4:14-17: *"Look, you're all my children; I'm your father. But I love you, and you are dear to me."* Here Paul puts forth the two essential truths that we need to communicate to others: first, understand that there is a structure of authority, and second, show love (respect) in our words and actions. These two things can coexist even though this goes against the culture of so many organizations today. To be successful, they need to! There is a grace involved in expressing your authority in a way in which people will kindly receive it and honor you. What is honor? I'd like to look at it in this way: honor others by taking an "honor look" at their life to see how you can make it better and not worse. I mean, after you connect with someone, they should be better than they were before you interacted with them. Make every interaction meaningful and purposeful. Be intentional about making sure that before you walk away from interacting with someone, they are not damaged but encouraged, motivated, and inspired to be better. So, commit to investing in people every time to create a positive culture. This will naturally cause them to respect you because they know that you respect and honor them too, and you are not trying to hold them back or waste their time. Go ahead and spark the change!

"It is better to lead from behind and to put others in front, especially when you celebrate victory when nice things occur. You take the front line when there is danger. Then people will appreciate your leadership."

– Nelson Mandela

FIVE

NOW AND LATER

BLOOM

Not only is it important to know how to treat others so that the interactions will promote a more positive culture, but it is also just as important to know, share, and pursue the foundational statements that define the organization's current position and future aspirations. These statements also have an impact on culture. This chapter will provide information about defining your organization, making your vision known, and establishing a plan that details how everyone fits into the overall success of the organization.

Defining Your Organization

When I was a little girl, I loved eating candy called, "Now and Later." I remember reciting a popular slogan, which included the words, "*Eat some now and save some for later*." The candy was extremely good, and I purchased it often at the neighborhood "Candy Lady." But the point I really want to make is that organizations must know what they are *now* and what they desire to become *later*. This information should be shared with all stakeholders. Doing so helps to maintain focus and could possibly eliminate some of the toxic behavior that may occur when individuals are idol, sidetracked and not focused on the mission and vision of the organization.

The mission statement describes what an organization is now, and the vision statement describes what the organization is aspiring to become. Moreover, the mission statement is where you define why your organization exists in the first place. In determining your mission, ask yourself the question, "Why do I feel called to start this organization?" or "Why do I feel called to this area?" Your mission statement is essential because it helps you set those goals to execute or accomplish your vision. The Bible states, *"Where there is no vision, the people perish: but he that keepeth the law, happy is he"* (Proverbs 29:18). When you have a clear vision of your final accomplishment, you have defined how you measure your success along the way; you are also able to set goals that will propel you on the path to your destination. You may not be the founder of the organization, but your role as a leader matters in carrying out the mission and working towards the vision. More importantly, you should know the mission and vision of your organization and ensure that those working with you are familiar with them as well. Below are a few examples of vision and mission statements.

Sample Mission Statement 1: *To make believers out of the unbelievers...and disciples out of believers.*

NOW AND LATER

Sample Vision Statement 1: *To build a devoted family of followers of Christ that worships God, shares Christ's hope and love, and ministers to each other's needs.*

Sample Mission Statement 2: *To become the main company of the world in the car's products and services.*

Sample Vision Statement 2: *We are a global, diverse family with a proud inheritance, providing exceptional products and services.*

Making Your Vision and Mission Known

Remember that vision is where you are going; mission is who you are and what you are doing right now. When we continue carrying out our mission daily, it contributes to our longer-term vision. A good example would be one of the large computer companies that had a vision of seeing a computer in every home. Their mission was to provide quality computers to consumers. It was a bold vision back then because computers were expensive and not many people could afford one. Guess what happened with this vision? The company had to change the vision because costs came down drastically and now most people have a computer at home. This company was forced to go and recast their vision. Things are going to change, and flexibility is vital.

You have to know your vision and be diligent in your mission to get things done. I don't mind saying it repeatedly because there are times when you're going to have to remind yourself and others where you are going and what you are doing now. It's easy to get off track but keeping these two things close to your heart will keep you laser-focused on your goals and help others to grow and develop. Doing so will also help you to avoid some pitfalls that sometimes come with interacting unacceptably with others.

You would be surprised, but I've found in my time teaching Bloom Leadership that not many people can tell me the vision, mission, and core values of their organization when I ask. I urge you to be ready to answer these questions. Have these foundational statements readily on your tongue at a moment's notice so that you become fully committed to them. One way to accomplish this is to have the foundational statements posted throughout your organization, on correspondence, and on your website. Make it visible to everyone everywhere. Then not only will you see it so often that you will always remember it, but it will also remind everyone else of it. We must constantly be aware of our mission and vision because they define who and what we are as an organization. People within and outside of the organization need to be aware of it, too. What about your core values now that you've memorized your mission and vision? These are easier. These are the values that drive every action behind your vision and mission and that undergird our calling to be successful leaders and earn the respect of others. Some of these values are love, honesty, integrity, etc. It will be challenging to fulfill your vision and mission if you do not make a commitment to upholding your core values in every interaction.

A few years ago, I had an opportunity to help an organization with assessment planning. In talking with leadership and reviewing the organization's overall strategy, I discovered that there was more to it than completing assessments. For one thing, there was no vision statement. Furthermore, the organization did not operate under guiding or core values so necessary to ensure that everyone in the organization was modeling appropriate behavior when carrying out their mission. I also noticed that there were many instances of toxic interactions that impacted the culture negatively. It was almost like a huge elephant in the room that everyone walked around instead of trying to move in order to avoid conflict.

> *Remember that vision is where you are going; mission is who you are and what you are doing right now.*

Now, the company needed a total revamp of their foundational value system that would necessitate a change of culture. The good thing was that the leaders were ready for change, and that made the job of trying to shift from a negative culture to a more positive culture possible. Not only is it necessary for the leaders to desire change, but they must model the change, expect to see change, and address actions that conflict with desired change. The steps taken were as follows:

- Developed a vision statement and revamped the mission statement
- Developed core values after deliberation by management and team leaders
- Conducted an assessment planning workshop with the entire organization to make sure everyone knew the vision, mission, and core values

- Allowed members and leaders to provide feedback about the goals and objectives of the organization
- Discussed the importance of unity (interactions) within the organization

The teaching on unity was an integral part of the assessment planning session to ensure that members understood that a positive culture and interactions were just as important as setting goals and carrying out the mission. Every member received the same lesson on unity so there was a corporate understanding of what was expected. Since the completion of the workshop, the organization has posted the vision, mission, and core values for all stakeholders to constantly view at the physical location, on the website, and on social media. The members of the organization can easily quote the vision, mission, and core values and there is a stronger sense of connection and community. There is also a common goal about where the organization is going and how they will interact with each other as they strive to get there. Is the organization still experiencing challenges in some areas? Yes. However, leaders are better prepared to face those challenges when they have a team of people who understand the organization's foundational statements and are eager to help carry them out. This is a true testament to what can happen when there are clear expectations not only about meeting goals, but also about the treatment of people in the process of meeting goals.

Establishing a Plan

In addition to establishing the foundational statements that define the organization, it is pertinent to also establish a plan that outlines how the day-to-day operations will be carried out in excellence. It involves the details – the what, when, and who. Leadership, those who lead and follow, is included in the plan. Every organization should have skilled leaders to lead the process of both defining the organization and managing and developing others to achieve success. Organizations must also have skilled followers who provide input regarding the overall plan of the organization and assist in implementing the established plans. According to Henri Fayol, there are four main areas of management that must be addressed to operate effectively and efficiently. The four areas of management are planning, leading, organizing, and control/evaluation.

BLOOM

1. **Planning**: This is the base step of writing out both of your statements and setting goals and objectives that will help you realize them. We need to plan before we do anything, or we will find ourselves wandering aimlessly. A solid plan will keep us on the upward path we need to achieve our goals. *Note: Members of the organization are more focused when there is a plan before them that helps in directing their attitude and behavior. Allowing input from stakeholders at all levels increases morale and innovation.*

2. **Leading**: This step involves communicating your vision and mission to those you work with, motivating them along the way, and continually reminding them why you are doing what you are doing. This includes supervising, mentoring, and delegating, among others. You are the go-to person for others in your organization. Live out your mission and vision statement to lead by example! *Note: Allowing others to also lead by delegating responsibility and asking for input is a way to help others develop and grow.*

3. **Organizing**: This step involves setting up your organization's structure and defining the job responsibilities. In addition, this step deserves as much time as it takes to perfect because your organization's structure will determine how smoothly your objectives can be met. Ensuring everyone is in a role that suits them best and serves your organization's needs in the most efficient manner possible will help to attain your goals. *Note: Don't be afraid to set up your organization outside of traditional centralized structures. When more people are empowered to get involved in decision-making, the benefit is two-fold: less burnout of leaders and the development of more people who are skilled to carry out responsibilities.*

4. **Evaluating**: In this phase, you develop the policies and procedures that will fuel your organization and you will regularly evaluate progress along the way. No matter how flexible and easygoing you may need to be, boundaries are always necessary to have a healthy balance of authority. Policies and procedures help to keep those boundaries in check. Regular evaluation of your organization is crucial because it allows you to take an honest look at things to see where you can adjust and foster growth. *Note: When evaluating policies and procedures, allow everyone to have a voice and value their feedback. Of course, you may not be able to implement*

every suggestion, but you may help boost morale and commitment by valuing how others feel and what they have to say.

For the four areas to be a success, everyone must know THE PLAN! It's all about the transition. To build momentum and create the competitive advantage you desire, leaders and followers must work together and realize each other's importance. This will be a catalyst to your growth and brand awareness, both of which will result in more customers/members. Try not to think of followers as people beneath you, but rather as partners who you need at your side to see the mission and vision through. Teamwork is critical, and great collaboration demands that you work alongside others, instead of watching them work for you.

Your plan will flow from the vision of the organization. As you follow these steps and lead the people crucial to your organization, you will continuously be adjusting how you do things to take your vision to its greatest potential. Plans must be flexible and thorough, and failure should be seen as part of the learning process. Understand that some of the best projects are birthed from failure. Seeing how something *does not* work can often have a way of showing you what *will* work. Never be so prideful that you cannot adapt when needed. Complacency will undoubtedly lead to your growth being stunted and your organization growing stagnant. Many leaders have fallen victim to pride as it is not so easily overcome and can unravel even the most excellent plans.

I want to take just a moment to mention that even religious organizations must plan in order to be successful. Two significant misconceptions exist when it comes to planning and churches. The first is that churches do not have to plan strategically like a business, and all that is needed is just to follow the leading of the Holy Spirit. Of course, as Christians, we must follow the Spirit's leading, and our planning should incorporate that! But churches must also plan, following the goals set forth by their vision and mission statement. So, planning will drive both *vision and mission* within your organization. Your vision needs to be what success looks like to your church. Craft your vision while thinking through what you will ultimately like your church to become. Remember that your mission will describe your church as it now stands, perhaps including details such as your target demographics, reach, and services. Just think about it: your organization's mission may not be

> *Organizations must also have skilled followers who provide input regarding the overall plan...*

the same as the church down the road. They might be called to focus on prison ministry, and you might be called to serve a specific county or region. You need to plan to find success in your unique calling. When members come together as one body, churches will be able to experience more success in spreading the Gospel and meeting the needs of God's people. Paul states, *"For as the body is one and hath many members, and all the members of that one body, being many, are one body: so also is Christ"* (1 Corinthians 12:12). God has given us different gifts and abilities, and we can make a greater impact in the world when the gifts are used collaboratively, instead of in comparison to or competition with each other. This holds true for any type of organization, be it religious, corporate, community based, etc.

Collaboration vs. Comparison

Think practically about the analogy that Paul poses about the body. Let's say that you are a hand. Our hands are crucial to our operations, allowing us to fulfill many tasks. But most of us do not realize the limitations of having to function with only one hand. If you are the hand, and you are not working in sync with the other hand and the rest of the body, the overall work of the Kingdom is hindered. Do not be the one who causes that to happen. Instead, submit yourself to being part of the body. Set goals and develop a strategy to meet your stated plans and not the plans of others. If you do not develop that strategy to hold yourself accountable, it will be impossible to meet your goals. Ensure that your goals are realistic and attainable, or else you will find a lot of frustration along the way. Furthermore, create goals that start small and get bigger and work towards growth at a manageable pace. Finally, give yourself grace. Sometimes you'll achieve your goals perfectly, and other times you may be a little or a lot off. That is natural but be encouraged that every misstep is an opportunity to grow.

Remember you are the one who defines your success. By developing your vision, you now have a template by which to measure your success. You can see how well you are accomplishing the goals set forth by your mission statement and how they are serving your vision. Nobody else can determine your success but you and the vision that has been established. Don't waste time comparing yourself or your organization to those around you. Just focus solely on what God has led you to accomplish. If you compare yourself to someone else's definition of success, you will likely experience great discouragement. Don't allow the enemy to get in your way and pit you against a "competitor." Stick to your vision and be reminded of the importance of what you are doing. Revisiting your vision and praying over the reasons you developed it in the first place will reinvigorate your purpose and give you renewed motivation to continue.

Some people within your organization need the same motivation to continue the work. They have significant talents given from God that they are not utilizing. This occurs for a variety of reasons, but it typically stems from their confidence being dented by toxic leadership from the past, a lack of progress, and an overall sense of failure. Perhaps they tried to use their skills before in an organization and things failed. They are now scared to try again. This is where outstanding leaders can make a remarkable difference in affirming their ability. Share your vision and mission and let them know that their skills hold significant value within your organization. This will be a catalyst in sparking their motivation and passion for their abilities once again. This type of leadership style inspires people, allowing them to accomplish great things. As a leader in your organization, you have a responsibility of inspiring and motivating others to use their gifts. Bloom Leadership is all about leaders committing to the flourishing of others. It is leadership with the intention of mentoring guiding others, rather than merely supervising, commanding, and directing them.

You have to create the right climate for people to thrive in collaboration with you. You must realize, though, not every person adapts to every climate. There are also those times when a specific place is not for a particular individual, no matter how favorable the environment. That's okay! It happens, and you must handle these circumstances politely and respectfully so that the necessary adjustments to create a more positive and ideal environment can be made.

"Leadership is unlocking people's potential to become better."

– Bill Bradley

PART III

Moving Beyond Challenges

SIX

OVERCOMING OFFENSES

BLOOM

Contrary to what many believe, not every interaction we experience in our organizations will be positive. Unfortunately, some people, who do not honor the concepts of a positive culture, will attempt to offend, disrespect, sabotage, lie or abuse others. It does not matter if you are a leader or a follower; you will have some type of negative interaction along your journey and being prepared will help you get over the disappointment and move forward.

Bloom Leadership includes ideal or positive behaviors that leaders and followers should carry out in an organization; however, there are times, as mentioned previously, when interactions and attitudes are not so positive. Some followers may find it challenging to follow a leader's guidance or may not want to be developed for growth, and some leaders may be insecure about their abilities and hinder the growth of others. Whatever the case, collaborating with others to achieve a common goal won't always go smoothly, and at some point along the way, we'll find ourselves facing a potential offense. This chapter is intended to help both leaders and followers understand offenses and provide strategies for getting past them.

Don't Take the Bait of Offense

It is impossible to avoid offenses, but we must not let our emotions rule our behavior. It may not be the sole reason to leave an organization or group. When I've experienced offenses in the past, sometimes, I felt led to stay, and other times, I felt it in my heart to leave. Perhaps God is trying to work on something in you as you go through the experience. Or perhaps, He is trying to use that particular situation to pull you out, and you need to run and not look back. It is best for you to look to the Holy Spirit for discernment in these matters; so, pray for guidance.

Someone once said that saying yes to offense is like your drinking Clorox and hoping that it kills someone else. The only person you are hurting is yourself. You must get rid of it for your own sake. It will eat you up from the inside out and cause toxicity in your life.

Matthew 18:7 reads, *"Woe unto the world because of offenses!"* Merriam Webster's definition of "offense" is *something that causes a person to be hurt or angry.* Being angry is not sinful in itself but dwelling on and giving in to your anger is sinful (See Ephesians 4:26). The New Testament Greek word for offense is *skandalōn*, which can be defined as *a movable stick or trigger of a trap*. If you've ever seen a rat trap, the cheese is not the offense. The cheese is the bait – the bait that causes you to say yes to being offended. The bait is pride, your ego, selfishness, vanity, or anger. So, are you going to stay mad for twenty years because of these things or even seek revenge? Once you say yes to the bait, the offense will trap and immobilize you, preventing you from freely moving forward to pursue your purpose. Yes, walking in offense will affect you in a negative way – it starts in your mind and thoughts, then moves to your heart and emotions; and for some, it can also affect your physical health.

Resisting the bait of offense so that you will not be trapped is easier when you walk according to the Word and allow the Holy Spirit to help you. Counter offenses with forgiveness, humility, and connectedness. *"For our struggle is not against flesh and blood, but against the rulers, against the authorities, against the powers of this dark world and against the spiritual forces of evil in the heavenly realms"* (Ephesians 6:12). You have to remember that the enemy will use whoever he can, so fight against him by learning to forgive, learning to love, and by learning to let go of the offense. We all need the power of the Holy Ghost operating through the Word to walk in love. Take a moment to meditate on these scriptures:

1. *"Love your enemies"* (Matthew 5:44). You have to love EVERYONE, even those who speak ill of you.

2. *"Bless them that curse you"* (Matthew 5:44). You can bless others with your words when you talk to them or about them to others in a positive manner.

3. *"Do good to them that hate you"* (Matthew 5:44). You can do good to people from a distance and not necessarily in their presence. Allow the Holy Spirit to lead you on what your "do good" needs to look like.

4. *"Pray for them which despitefully use you, and persecute you"* (Matthew 5:44). You are God's child, and He cares about you. Praying for those who offend you does them good.

The bottom line is that we have to forgive others. Forgiveness was so crucial to Jesus that with His dying breath He remembered to pray for His executioners, *"Father, forgive them; for they know not what they do"* (Luke 23:34). He forgave the people who caused Him such pain because He was not going to carry any unforgiveness or bitterness to the grave. Let us be like Jesus in our homes, in our churches, and even in our organizations.

The Path to Forgiveness

The condition of our heart matters when it comes to whether we are going to walk in forgiveness and live in the peace that was promised or turn bitter because of unforgiveness and discouragement. It is also the condition of our heart that determines how fruitful we will be (See Mark 4). Sometimes we pretend and avoid dealing with how we truly feel in our hearts. I call it *Christian camouflage.* We act as if everything is normal, but we are really harboring resentment and bitterness in our hearts. Our feelings may be towards an organization itself or a person who has somehow wronged us. We must learn to truly forgive so we can be fruitful and not allow the root of bitterness to be lodged deep within. How do you remove it? Let's look at Scripture for guidance.

> *It is the condition of our heart that determines how fruitful we will be...*

Luke 17:1 reads, *"Then He said to the disciples, 'It is impossible that no offenses should come, but woe to him through whom they do come!'"* There's no doubt about it; offenses will surely come. Our workplaces and churches are not exempt from this. Offenses are painful and can make us resentful and discouraged. Is there any benefit to them? One benefit I find in offense, even with all of the pain, is that it brings us to our knees. It is humbling and makes us reach out to God in response. When things are always going well, we don't pray as much. Difficulties challenge us and help us to grow. God will cause a bad or offensive situation to work for our good. Besides, the Bible states, *"And we know that all things work together for good to them that love God, to them who are the called according to his purpose."* (Romans 8:28).

In the next verse in Luke, Jesus turns to those who are the cause of offense, *"It were better for him that a millstone were hanged about his neck, and he cast into the sea than that he should offend one of these little ones"* (Luke 17:2). Notice, Jesus does not say that this will happen if you offend the leader. Instead, He said if you offend even the little ones. Therefore, do not only watch your words and behavior

OVERCOMING OFFENSES

with people who are in higher positions. Instead, respect everyone regardless of their title. Protecting those who others deem weak and vulnerable should be a top priority. These individuals, without saying a word to anyone, may experience untold damage because of mistreatment in organizations. Believe it or not, the abuse may leave the individuals traumatized and discouraged for a lifetime. As leaders, we must take offenses seriously and ensure everyone in our organization understands the expectations regarding how others should be treated.

Jesus continues, *"Take heed to yourselves: If thy brother trespass against thee, rebuke him; and if he repents, forgive him"* (Luke 17:3). When I think about the word "trespass," I think of the Lord's Prayer I learned as a child: *"And forgive us our trespasses, as we forgive those who trespass against us"* (Matthew 6:12). This scripture carries a lot of weight because it makes us ask ourselves, "Have we really forgiven those who have wronged us?" If not, how can we expect God's forgiveness in return? Let our mindset be, "Lord, let me forgive others the same way that I've been forgiven. Let me also not be bitter or revengeful as I move forward to do your will."

We need to model forgiveness in our own lives if we expect to be forgiven in return. When we are offended in our organizations, it is not an option to forgive. We are commanded to forgive. We do have an option about what happens after we forgive. Do we forgive and walk away? Do we forgive and stay connected? Do we forgive and allow the situation to be handled by the system of the law? If we are in a leadership position, do we forgive and reprimand the person? How you move forward depends on how you are led by the Holy Spirit and how you are guided by the rules and culture of your organization. Are we being honest about how we feel in our hearts when we interact with others? We need to put off our Christian camouflage.

We don't want to be one person at work or at church, and then a different one at home. That is not how God desires us to be. If we are not willing to forgive, we can't be genuine. We will live a double life, and we will not be able to walk the path laid out for us free of unnecessary burdens. In verse 4, Jesus says, *"And if he trespass against thee seven times in a day, and seven times in a day turn again to thee, saying, I repent; thou shalt forgive him"* (Luke 17:4). Jesus is emphasizing the fact that our forgiveness needs to be towards all men and we may have to forgive again and again. Only God can enable us to forgive others the way that He forgives us. Therefore, ask the Holy Spirit to help you to walk in forgiveness as sometimes the pain of the wrongdoing is so great that your heart is reluctant to extend mercy and forgiveness to the offender. Verse 5 states, *"And the apostles said unto the Lord, Increase our faith"* (Luke 17:5). We have to believe that God will help us when we find it difficult to deal with offense. If we trust Him with things like our finances, where we will live, and our healing, why can't we believe God for our ability to forgive from our heart? Why can't we apply our faith in forgiving others? In other words, why can't we forgive despite how our heart feels and trust God to heal us from the pain?

Some people have admitted to me that they have not spoken to another family member in years. When asked about what happened, they don't even remember what caused them to fall out of fellowship in the first place. I have certainly been there myself. It's all because we have allowed bitterness to take root and take control of our lives. We must continually pray for the Lord to increase our faith. Verse 6 reads, *"And the Lord said, If ye had faith as a grain of mustard seed, you might say unto this sycamine tree, Be thou plucked up by the root, and be thou planted in the sea; and it should obey you"* (Luke 17:6). It takes only mustard-seed faith to pluck out the root of bitterness from within us.

We have to pray to wholeheartedly receive that faith to speak to the mountain of unforgiveness and tell it to move. I was always curious why this particular scripture used the image of a sycamore tree instead of a mountain, *"you might say unto this sycamine tree."* I had never heard it this way. It is because a tree has deep roots. Bitterness in our lives tends to take root and burrow deep. You can just cut the tree, but it doesn't solve the problem. You are merely masking it. To truly eliminate the issue once and for all, you must pluck it out, roots and all. Once out of the ground, the roots can no longer nourish the problems. They will dry up without their source of strength.

It's similar to how people attempt to treat acne by using cosmetic products. It is merely covering up the surface and not dealing with the root of the problem. It doesn't go deep enough. I knew someone who kept going back to the doctor because of an inexplicable pain. No matter what the doctor did, he could not figure out what was causing the pain. This was because the issue was much deeper than they could diagnose. It wasn't on the surface; they had to make a decision and be willing to look deeper. Are you willing to pluck up bitterness in your life that continues to torment you? It will require an in-depth process of searching your heart and exercising your faith to allow God to heal you from the pain so that you are able to live a life full of joy that will compel others to want to know Christ. It's time for you to be free!

OVERCOMING OFFENSES

Keeping Your Mind at Peace

In addition to forgiving others, we also need to keep laser-focused on God to find the peace necessary to dispel what I like to call the *woulda, coulda, shoulda* syndrome. This is when you obsessively revisit a situation in your mind and think of how it *could* have played out. "If only…" you keep thinking. But that all happened in the past and there is no way of reversing it. Only God can deliver you from this torment of wishing you had acted differently. Isaiah 26:3 reads, *"You will keep him in perfect peace, Whose mind is stayed on You Because he trusts in You."* We must keep our minds centered on God. We must trust in Him to deliver us from unhealthy thoughts because He is the only One who can give us that perfect peace.

The enemy knows our predicament and is quick to attack our mind because he wants to destroy our peace as he is a thief. Have you ever been happy one minute, but very suddenly, a thought comes to your mind that ruins your entire mood? That's the enemy at work. You can confront it by declaring, "No matter what I'm going through, I have peace. It doesn't matter what the enemy tries to throw at me. I know that God has got me. I can counter his attacks with the Word because I keep it close to my heart." Learn new scriptures every day. Learn a new song, based on scripture, to sing to Jesus when you need to replace negative thoughts.

On a personal note, I thought that I would stay married to the same person for the rest of my life – until we started having serious marital issues and eventually got a divorce. It sent me into a loop, and I'll never forget the shame and hardship I endured over that period. Those hours late at night were the hardest. But at the same time, I learned how to use spiritual weapons and one of them was praise. I remember singing, "Oh What Grace to Trust Him More" all of the time. Through those lyrics, God's presence flooded me with hope. God reassured me that I could get through the situation. I learned how to replace negative thoughts with positive ones. I had to be intentional about it and cast out the thoughts sent by the enemy. I started writing books and songs. I have written close to ten books now and over seventy-five songs. I wrote most of these when I was going through some very difficult times in my life.

Peace comes from God and because it is not based on my situation or my challenges; the peace that I have does not fluctuate up and down like a rollercoaster. Instead, God's peace, that is made available through Jesus Christ, is unmovable, unchanging, and consistent. We may change, our situations may change, but the peace of God – the peace that God gives us – does not change. So, when we are faced with difficult situations in organizations, in our family, or in our relationships, we can stand and endure because we have God's peace, and we can come out of the fire not being consumed or smelling like the smoke of our situation. We should be thankful that God loved us enough to send His only begotten Son, Jesus Christ, to redeem us back to Him and provide us with His peace that enables us to live victoriously in all situations.

Looking at Negative Experiences Differently

Negative experiences can be damaging emotionally – causing stress, anxiety, discouragement, disappointment, etc. Disappointment is a low feeling that one may have for an appointed and short-term period. On the other hand, discouragement is more serious in that it requires self-encouragement or outside encouragement to bring about the healing necessary to move forward. Discouragement also causes people to not want to try again or even if they do try, not give it their best. Additionally, it is essential to address discouragement immediately to prevent stagnation.

I had to get over some negative experiences in my career in order to keep moving forward. Those experiences caused me to turn to and trust God more for my survival and future success. I had to develop what I call *weeble wobble* mentality. You see, the Weeble Wobble is a toy that, after being pushed down, comes right back up quickly. It didn't stay down. And like this toy, we also do not have to stay down after we have had some negative experiences in our organizations or relationships. God is there to help us get back up and go back in again.

Admittedly, it is easier to talk about wonderful things that happen on the job or to talk about a great career path that we see ahead. But what about the not-so-great experiences that we've had…the ones that took the wind out of our sails and left us in a seemingly stand-still position without anyone to trust and lean on but God Almighty…the experiences that left us heartbroken and, in some cases, ashamed – whether it was our fault or not. It is downright difficult to talk about those experiences. But just like the positive experiences in our life, those negative experiences have helped to sharpen the very person we have become.

OVERCOMING OFFENSES

And, just as it takes both a positive and negative terminal to charge a battery, causing a car to start and go forward, it also takes both positive and negative experiences in the journey of life to cause us to keep moving forward. I don't care how pretty a car looks on the outside and the interior, without a charge to the negative terminal on the battery, the car "ain't going nowhere." Our negative experiences cause us to appreciate when things are going well and, in my case, they helped me to go from selfish to selfless mode, being aware of my treatment of others, and understanding the importance of reaching outside of myself to serve those who are hurting. I came to understand God's amazing grace. He showed me through my negative experiences – in the workplace and in relationships – that I was nothing without Him, and with Him, I could press through anything. I learned to trust God more during my negative experiences, so yes...they also helped me to move forward and to become a better me.

> ...if you are in a dark place, it does not always indicate that you are in the wrong place.

I want you to understand that if you are in a dark place, it does not always indicate that you are in the wrong place. As an illustration, when a seed is planted, it is put in a dark place with dirt all around it. It is alone in the space designated for its growth. To this end, being planted doesn't feel good or look good. Notice I referred to the seed being planted and not buried. When something is buried, it does not have the capacity to come up out of the dirt and the intention is to leave it there. But when you are planted, God has equipped you with the substance you need on the inside of you to rise up out of the dirt that was necessary for your growth. It's in YOU! Nobody will have to pick you up as God will get the credit and the glory for your breaking through the barrier.

All you have to do is be willing to receive the nourishment that He provides...the sunlight, the water, the nutrients. To me, these represent the Savior, the Holy Spirit, and the Word. They make all the difference in being planted instead of buried. When others throw dirt on you...when they bring up your past or try to make it difficult for you to get ahead, and call you everything but a child of God, what they don't understand is that they are actually helping you to grow. Soon, you will begin to bloom out of the very dirt that was meant to hinder you. Why? Because you are learning to rely on the shield of faith to fend off those fiery darts, the helmet of salvation to keep your mind centered on Christ, and the sword of the

Spirit to fight back with the Word of God (See Ephesians 6:10-18). So, know that you have been planted for a purpose. Even though it may be dark and there is dirt all around you, be encouraged. It will not last forever. In due time, you're coming up! Say this: I'm coming up! I'm coming up! I'm coming up!

I heard a prominent preacher say that you are no kind of leader until you have some wounds. I agree wholeheartedly. The scars you possess have value. Your scars are evidence that you are a survivor, that you can persevere, that you can press in. The scars show that you rose above your circumstance, and that you still have an opportunity to do more and grow! Every negative situation you have been through has equipped you for where you are today…it taught you how to move or where not to move as you go forward.

So, say this, "The Bible says that all things work together for my good. The good and the bad are working for my good. I bless the Lord! I accept my wounds and no longer walk in denial and shame. I own who I am and know that I am better because of what I've been through. In all things, I give God all the praise and the glory belongs to Him!"

How can you tell others that they can make it through unless you yourself have made it through some things? How can you tell others that they too can rise out of the dirt after being planted for a season to later bloom with beauty? After going through tribulation, know that you can be used to sound the trumpet of victory! Hallelujah! Let the words of Jesus inspire you, "*Verily, verily, I say unto you, except a corn of wheat fall into the ground and die, it abideth alone: but if it die, it bringeth forth much fruit*" (John 12:24). Allow people to see and to hear your testimony so that they can be inspired to also persevere through tribulation. If people think that you have always looked like a shiny nickel, how can they be encouraged by your life? Humble yourself and allow people to see your scars – your wounds – so that they can give God the glory when they see your transformation. What you have gone through is like gold that has been refined.

It bears repeating that everyone in an organization will have an unfavorable or negative interaction with another person at some point. Good news. You can recover. Do not allow discouragement to cripple you and cause you not to move forward or go back in, which may mean resolving the matter that caused the negative interaction in the first place (apology, meeting, compromise, mediation, etc.). Conversely,

OVERCOMING OFFENSES

your *going back in* may look a little different. It may be in another position or department. It may be starting your own business or connecting with another organization. Nevertheless, you can have joy again working with others in a climate that is best for you to grow. You have to look inside of yourself to know who you really are and what motivates and brings you joy. Ask yourself, "Am I living according to my purpose?" If the answer is no, then maybe it's time to take a closer look at yourself so that you may go back in with purpose and fulfillment. Allow the Holy Spirit to lead you in knowing if you should stay or walk away from a situation to pursue purpose or to avoid further disappointments.

Now that you have read this book, make a decision to *go back in* as a better leader, ready to help others BLOOM because of your transformation, or go back in as a better follower (at any level), ready to be nurtured to BLOOM because you have been healed from past disappointments. Whatever the case, the 'garden culture' of your organization will be filled with beautiful flowers that enhance lives for the better.

"True leadership is not about power; it's about empowerment."

– Myles Monroe

Epilogue

The ultimate goal of this book was to teach leaders and followers how to respectfully interact with each other towards a common goal. Additionally, this book aimed to teach them how to recognize interactions that are less than ideal and how to move beyond them. Leaders must inspire followers towards the vision – identifying and meeting needs along the way – and followers must move towards the vision while receiving guidance and participating in the process achieving goals. In everything, we need to look to Jesus' example. As I close out this book, I want to revisit the teachings of Jesus, which serve as foundational principles pertinent to transforming organizational culture.

Teach Like Jesus

In leadership, Jesus gives the ultimate illustration of what a good leader is. He chose twelve men in one day but led them in deep discipleship over the next three years. He had an intense level of commitment to them that we need to emulate as much as possible. Jesus chose men to follow Him so that He could make them fishers of men who would tell others about Him (See Matthew 4:19). He tells them this right away, giving them a clear expectation of what their mission was. He brought them into His circle and nurtured them, investing in their growth every step of the way. Even during the times that the disciples quarreled or did not do things the way that they should have, Jesus both expected and reinforced the type of culture which He was working so hard to cultivate. Everyone needs redirection sometimes, and Jesus was quick to give it. He redirected them when they would miss their step, often by using parables to impart wisdom in a way that was not harsh.

Jesus was also the ultimate example of how we are to interact with others. Yes, He shared the vision and the mission with His disciples, but He also invested a lot of time and energy into His relationship with them. In addition, He led by example in teaching them how to treat each other and those they were called to reach. *Therefore, treating people well along the way was just as important as completing the mission.* In other words, Jesus shared *what* they should do and then taught them *how* to carry out their mission.

So, we understand that Jesus taught about the mission and treatment of others in His examples to the disciples. Did the vision, mission, core values, and discipleship that He passed on to them allow them to be successful in their vision of spreading Christianity all over the globe? Let's look at the facts. In their time, the disciples carried out the Great Commission by spreading the gospel, and the Lord added to the

Kingdom thousands of souls daily (See Acts 2:47). Today, Christianity is the largest religion worldwide, with billions of people who have proclaimed Christ. I am sure you would agree that they were pretty successful.

With so many Christians today, it is remarkable to remember that it all started with a great leader. Jesus accomplished this mighty feat, starting with only the twelve disciples. Put this into perspective. If Jesus leads by example and wants us to emulate Him, what can we accomplish with those He has entrusted us with today? What kind of impact do you hope to have? How long will it last even when you are no longer here? Start putting together your plan that will address all of these questions. This will allow you to be a significant culture change agent. You will see authentic, impactful, and powerful progress when people know how to treat each other and work together as one body to accomplish the mission.

The Five-Step Process of Training

Since Jesus took a tremendous amount of time teaching the disciples about carrying out the Great Commission and interacting with others according to the Great Commandment, we too, as leaders, should take the necessary steps to ensure that training in the areas of productivity and culture is a vital part of our daily operations. Additionally, we must be willing to teach or train others for the purposes of improvement and development. Below are Kathy Howard's 5M steps of leadership development and understanding the process of training within an organization.

1. **Modeling:** Modeling is leading by example. Be the kind of person in your organization that you desire others to be. It is that simple.

2. **Mentoring:** Take time with those you have committed to develop, helping them to set goals and provide them with constructive feedback. Also, allow them to practice what they have been taught based on your level of authority to do so.

3. **Monitoring:** Determine how you will keep track of the progress being made to ensure that the path and goals you have set together are being accomplished.

4. **Motivating:** Make yourself available from time to time to lend both a listening ear and an encouraging word, as well as to show your appreciation. Continually remind everyone of the mission of your organization and their critical role in carrying it out.

5. **Multiplying:** Look for leadership potential in people and cultivate those skills today so they can lead tomorrow! Naturally, there will come a time when new leadership is needed to support and carry on the work after you.

The Benefit of the Bloom

We have established that leadership is all about influence and that anyone can influence others, even if they are not in a formal position of authority. We also established that knowing how to interact with others to improve the culture at any level is vital for individuals to grow and flourish in the organization. We must take the utmost care in the way we treat others if we want to be successful in inspiring them towards vision, experiencing satisfaction, and providing excellence in service.

As a leader who nurtures another, you do not have to do all of the work yourself. As mentioned previously, leaders must be willing to delegate, which follows Jesus' example, *"And he saith unto them, Follow me, and I will make you fishers of men"* (Matthew 4:19). Have you ever felt overwhelmed because you had too much on your plate? If yes, learning how to provide opportunities for others through development and delegation may be the answer. I learned the art of delegation early in my life and I have also learned how to identify and encourage the potential in others. Moreover, I have taught the art of delegation to a number of leaders through coaching and at conferences. I have found that delegation, when used properly, can be a tool to help others grow.

I want to take you back to a time when I was in elementary school. I was the type of person who had to do everything myself because I wanted my work to be "perfect." I remember having to cut out drawings along the dotted lines while we worked together in a group. I had to be the one to cut the paper because I didn't trust anyone else at my table to stay on the dotted lines and cut the drawings out perfectly. This way of thinking did not last long as doing all the tedious work, without any help, was tiresome. I learned that doing everything yourself is not the way, and helping others is extremely important. It is one thing to cut out a drawing perfectly yourself, but it's an even better thing to help someone else do the same.

At different times in my life, I have been in positions where someone else had to let go of the scissors, so to speak, and allow me an opportunity to learn how to cut along the dotted lines. Some leaders were patient and guided me when I veered off the dotted lines just a bit, and there were other leaders who did not take the time to graciously and respectfully show me how to improve. Nonetheless, I grew and bloomed through it all and learned how to help others bloom and not be buried, with no hope of growth.

The little girl who eventually learned how to allow others an opportunity to try their hand at cutting along dotted lines and give a helping hand if needed, grew up to become the author of BLOOM, which inspires leaders to help others grow by following the example of Jesus Christ and others in the Bible – accepting, appreciating, admiring (respecting), advising, and advancing others to become a better version of themselves.

Know that there is beauty in the scars that you have received in your past, there is preparation in your seasons of being planted, and there is greater impact that comes as a result of your willingness to serve and develop others. Also know that others are being influenced by your leadership – all of it.

I pray that your garden (home, work, church, non-profit, community, etc.) will be filled with beautiful flowers because of your commitment to helping others…BLOOM.

Endnotes

The 5 M Plan to Develop Bible Study Leaders. by Kathy Howard. Unshakeable Faith for Life. Mar 16, 2015 | Discipleship, women's ministry. Retrieved from: https://www.kathyhoward.org/the-5-m-plan-bible-study-leaders/

Kram, K. E. (1983). Phases of the mentor relationship. *Academy of Management Journal*, 26, 608–625. https://doi.org/cq49

Resilient, Live a Happier Life Website. Retrieved from: https://resilientblog.co/inspirational/quotes-about-blooming/

"What Are the Four Basic Functions That Make Up the Management Process." Houston Chronicle. Retrieved from: http://smallbusiness.chron.com/four-basic-functions-make-up-management-process-23852.html

About the Author

Dr. C. D. Dudley's life encompasses all of these roles: author, songwriter, producer, philanthropist, adjunct professor, management consultant, publishing executive, leadership strategist, and licensed minister. She is the President and CEO of a multi-management operations firm that provides book publishing, music production, assessment planning, and professional development services. Additionally, she has created and offers seminars on leadership, delegation, assessment/vision planning, culture transformation, self-acceptance, etc.

Born in Georgia, Dr. Dudley holds a Bachelor of Business Administration degree in Management; a Master of Business Administration degree, graduating with the highest honors; and a Doctor of Education degree in Organizational Leadership. In spite of spending part of her childhood in one of the most notorious districts in Atlanta for gang activity, she relentlessly pursued her ambition with the support of family, friends, teachers, and spiritual leaders. With over 25 years of experience in post-secondary instruction and administration, she firmly believes in the value of life-long education.

Dr. Dudley has a passion for music and helping children excel. She is the founder of Judah Music & Dance Honors, which awards performing arts scholarships to deserving youth. She has written and produced over 70 songs for her children's programs. Dr. Dudley is the Executive Producer of the emerging, interactive, children's show, Bible Boogie LIVE as well as the founder of the Future Success Kids program that inspires elementary-school children to think early about their career options through a fun-filled and educational workbook and sing-along CD. She is also the lyricist for the Alma Mater at Georgia Piedmont Technical College.

As a champion for individuals from low-income households, Dr. Dudley is fully committed to philanthropic causes, including breast cancer awareness, homelessness support, early career exploration, and achieving self-sufficiency. Dudley has four children who fully support her in ministry. She loves traveling with her family and encouraging young people, through her various ministries, to know God and to hold on to His unchanging hand. Ever ready to share her testimony with others, she declares that she is a victor, not a victim, no longer bound by the events of her past but walking in newness of life with her Lord and Savior Jesus Christ.

Other Products & Services

Visit
www.mewellc.com
to order TODAY!

Note: To schedule a **BLOOM Leadership** seminar onsite/offsite for your organization or to schedule a **Tea with Dr. D. - Bloom Leader** interview, please complete the Contact Us form at **www.DrCDDudley.com**.

www.ingramcontent.com/pod-product-compliance
Lightning Source LLC
Chambersburg PA
CBHW051316110526
44590CB00031B/4374